GONE TO POT

CANNABIS: What every parent needs to know

by
Terry Hammond

"This is a very important and powerful book."

- *Marjorie Wallace CBE*
Hon Fellow RCPsych - Founder and CEO SANE.

How to use this book

This book is in five parts.

Part 1: Tells a very powerful story of the impact cannabis had on one family

Part 2: Explains why cannabis can be so dangerous

Part 3: A guide on how parents can help their children avoid cannabis

Part 4: What to do if your child develops a cannabis induced mental illness

Part 5: How cannabis affects all our lives

It has been written so the reader can 'dip' into the book to read a specific part relevant to their family situation. The book also incorporates 'Quick Response' codes, which are a type of barcode, commonly known as 'QR' codes. This enables the reader to easily access information straight from the website by using a smart phone or iPad. All the QR codes have been carefully chosen to help the reader to maximise their knowledge and understanding.

How do I use the QR links in this book?

Don't worry, it is not complicated: all you need is a smart phone or iPad.

1. Open up your phone as if you are going to take a photo and point the screen at the QR code.

2. You should not need to actually take the photo, the built in camara should automatically recognise the code, and the relevant website link should immediately appear on the screen.

3. To activate the website, touch the website link that appears on the screen and the relevant website should open.

4. If you experience problems, you may have an older phone; the easiest thing to do is to check with your phone provider, who should be able to advise you.

5. Even if you are unable to open the link, then don't worry, I have provided the actual web addresses of all the QR links so you can open them manually on your device.

Introduction

PART 1:

Chapter 1: The Boy I Used To Know - A Father's Story *17*

1. A Bolt from the Blue
2. The Worst Night of my Life
3. Hospitalisation
4. The Long Haul Begins
5. The Impact on Us
6. The Effects on my Daughter
7. His Non-Compliance
8. Self-Neglect
9. The Drinking
10. A Beacon of Hope
11. 20 Years On
12. The Future

PART 2:

Chapter 2: Understanding Cannabis and why it can be so Dangerous *36*

1. The Clue is in its Biological Make-Up
2. A Quick History of Cannabis
3. Cannabis as a Medicine
4. Can you Become Addicted to Cannabis?
5. Is Cannabis a 'Gateway' to Hard Drugs such as Heroin?
6. Is it Better to Vape or Smoke Synthetic Cannabis (Cannabinoids)?

7. Recent Moves to Decriminalise Cannabis
8. Cannabis-Induced Mental Illness Starts to Increase
9. Alarm Raised by Mental Health Staff and Parents
10. A False Dawn
11. UK Temporarily Decriminalises Cannabis
12. The Confusing Messages to the Public

Chapter 3: The Link Between Cannabis and Mental Illness *51*

1. Understanding Mental Illness
2. The Role our Genes Play
3. Social Factors
4. Lifestyle and Personal Choices
5. The Science Behind How Cannabis Affects the Functioning of the Brain

Chapter: 4: The Hard Evidence We Have Been Waiting For *60*

1. Research Published in the US 2017
2. European Research Published in the UK 2019
3. How Many People are Affected by Cannabis-Induced Psychosis?
4. Convincing the Public of the Hard Evidence

Chapter 5: Cannabis: A Public Health Emergency *67*

1. The Size of the Problem
2. The Fall and Rise of Cannabis
3. The Myth that Alcohol is Safer than Cannabis

PART 3:

Chapter 6: How Parents Can Help Their Children Stay Clear of Cannabis   *76*

1. Introduction
2. Understanding Why Your Child Would Want to Take Cannabis
3. When Do You Start Talking to Your Children About Drugs?
4. Tips for Engaging with Children on Drug Awareness
5. Dealing with Primary Schoolchildren (5-8)
6. What to Say to Your Pre-teen About Drugs (9-12 year olds)
7. Confronting the Issue of Drugs With Teenagers
8. Talking to Teenagers Who Have Not Tried Cannabis
9. Dealing With Teenagers Who Are Already Experimenting With Cannabis - The Warning Signs - What to Look For and When
10. Steps You Can Take
11. What Happens if My Teenage Child Refuses to Cooperate?
12. Summary

PART 4:

Chapter 7: What to do when Cannabis Takes Hold   *99*

1. The Warning Signs
2. The Steps You Can Take
3. Making the First Step to Getting an Assessment
4. Contacting Your GP
5. Once You Get an Appointment With Your GP
6. What Happens if You Are Told that Your Child Cannot be Treated Until They Stop Taking Cannabis?

7. What Happens When Your Child is Over 18 and Refuses to Cooperate?
8. Dealing with Children Under 18
9. Preparing for the CAMHS (Child and Adolescent Mental Health Services) Assessment
10. What happens after the Assessment?
11. Receiving a Diagnosis

Chapter 8: Treating Psychosis *113*
1. The Treatment Options
2. Non-Compliance
3. Self-Medication
4. Communicating With a Child Who is Refusing Medication
5. Getting a Second Opinion
6. Staying Involved

Chapter 9: Practical Things You Can Do To Help Matters *121*

1. Learn Not to Blame Yourself
2. Read Up on Your Child's Diagnosis and Treatment
3. Talk to Other Parents or Join a 'Carers Group'
4. Link Up With a Specialist Charity
5. Arrange for a Carers Assessment
6. Find out about Welfare Benefits
7. A Benefits Horror Story
8. Understanding How the System Works
9. Learn to be Proactive and Not to wait for the System to React
10. Dealing With Confidentiality
11. Parents Learning to Live with Psychosis

PART 5:

Chapter 10: How Cannabis Effects All Our Lives　　　*148*
1. The Hidden Impact of Cannabis
2. Cannabis Violence and Knife Crime
3. The Cost of Mental Illness
4. The Need to Raise Public Awareness
5. The Role the Education System has to Play
6. To Legalise or Not to Legalise
7. The Case To Legalise Cannabis for Recreational Use
8. The Case Against Legalising Cannabis for Recreational Use
9. Summary of Legalisation of Cannabis
10. My Views on Legalisation of Cannabis
11. If, in the Future, the UK Legalises Cannabis, What Should Future Legalisation Look Like?

Chapter 11: Final Reflection　　　*182*

Epilogue: When Hope Flowers　　　*185*

Appendix 1: The three basic components the government should include in any future legislation to legalise cannabis

Illustrations:
Fig 1: Reported Proportion of Adults Using Cannabis, 1996-2018, Age Groups 16-24 & 16-59
Fig 2: A single brain cell
Fig 3: The synapse gap
Fig 4: Pupils who have admitted to taking drugs
Fig 5: Number of drugs and type of drug taken in the last year by schoolchildren
Fig 6: Factors associated with taking drugs
Fig 7: Reported Proportion of Adults Using Cannabis, 1996-2018, Age groups 16-24 &16-59

Acknowledgements　　　*189*

Introduction

Cannabis is a 'time bomb' that few seemed to have heard go off. Thousands of young people are having their minds wrecked by this innocuous looking plant. As one teacher told me "It is not the smell of tobacco you smell behind the bicycle sheds these days it is cannabis". It's time parents, policy makers and politicians wake up and start to 'smell the pot'.

Cannabis - My First Concerns

"Can you see the TV in my eyes? Look closer and you will see my eyes are tuned into channel two; go on have a good look". I did look, but being careful not to go along with Justin's obvious delusions, and also being careful not to upset Justin (not his real name), I responded; "I can't see what you can see Justin, but I believe that is what you can see". Justin was a tall man in his thirties, his face was tired and haggard - his skin in poor condition and hair unkempt. He had recently been discharged from a psychiatric hospital and placed in a supported home I managed back in the early 1980s. Three years earlier, Justin put a brick through the window of a TV shop, jumped inside and sat amongst his 'friends'. He was arrested, put in prison, then later moved to a psychiatric hospital. As part of his rehabilitation he was placed in the care of the supported home. I rang the Community Psychiatric Nurse and told him what Justin had said to me. He agreed that he was starting to get delusional again and that he may have to go back into hospital - we later found cannabis in his room - Justin had a history of using cannabis, which went back to when he first became ill at university.

This was the first time I started to question whether cannabis might be linked to mental illness. I was responsible for overseeing fifteen houses providing homes for over 120 people, mostly with schizophrenia. I decided to do my own study by gently asking residents if they had ever taken cannabis. A small minority had and, worryingly, some were still using it, including Justin.

In the 70s and 80s cannabis was mostly considered a harmless recreation drug which hippies used to chill out at music festivals. When I raised the issue at the time, it was argued that there were far too many other factors to pin the blame on cannabis, there was little scientific evidence proving any such link (although unbeknown to me there was major research going on in Sweden) and besides, many psychiatric patients also drank, smoked heavily, often lived chaotic lives and sometimes used other illegal substances, so it was impossible to make a direct link. The issue continued to nag me for many years, but without any proper evidence there was little point in pushing it.

That was thirty-five years ago; thanks to modern science we now know with reasonable certainty that cannabis can lead to very serious mental health issues, such as schizophrenia and psychotic episodes. (We have also learned that it is particularly dangerous for teenagers, whose brains are still developing, and who are being exposed to far more powerful and dangerous strains of cannabis - commonly known as skunk.) Cannabis is the most popular illegal drug used by teenagers and has started to replace cigarette smoking. It is becoming more and more difficult for parents to shield their children from cannabis. Young people are being exposed to it at schools, colleges and socially. It is not uncommon to see them smoking it in parks after school and the smell of cannabis is increasingly permeating the streets of our inner cities. There is very strong evidence that cannabis can be addictive, and it can lead to more powerful drugs such as heroin – cannabis is most definitely a 'Gateway Drug' as many long-term drug addicts will admit.

Cannabis-induced psychosis amongst teenagers has substantially increased over the years. According to research reported in *The Psychiatry Lancet* (vol 6. 1 May 2019)[1] cannabis is now one of the biggest causes of first-time psychosis in South London; it accounts for a staggering 30% of new cases and 50% of new cases in Amsterdam - both cites having a reputation for high-potency cannabis being sold on the streets. Incidences of schizophrenia have more than doubled.

Cannabis has now become a major issue, affecting many thousands of teenagers every year who are ending up with serious mental health issues and for many, it will last a lifetime. At the same time governments around the world are looking to legalise cannabis; many have already done so for medical use, including the UK. The large multi-national companies are investing billions into developing and advertising cannabis-based health products, and are actively lobbying governments to legalise cannabis. Similar studies that have identified the dangers of cannabis have also shown that cannabis can have health benefits, particularly with pain relief.

The therapeutic value of cannabis has been known for centuries, as well as its mind-altering properties. So, the question arises, what do you say to your children when there are so many mixed messages about cannabis? On the one hand they are being told it can be dangerous, on the other hand governments are legitimising its use by legalising it, thus sending the green light to teenagers that it's ok to use.

---

[1] https://www.thelancet.com/journals/lanpsy/article/PIIS2215-0366(19)30048-3/fulltext (accessed: 27.06.20)

I hope this book will help parents to unravel this conundrum and help to give the whole family a far better understanding of this very complex plant. My prime objective is to highlight the considerable dangers cannabis can pose to young people. To give parents the confidence to talk about cannabis and drugs in general during those crucial pre-teen years. To enable parents to steer their teenage children away from cannabis which, sadly, most are likely to come across in their young lives. It may all seem a bit too daunting but, having researched models around the world, I am confident if parents take some very basic steps which are outlined in this book, they can make a substantial difference to their children's understanding of mind-altering drugs such as cannabis, and also empower their children to make an informed choice if they are ever tempted to experiment with cannabis.

Sadly, for many parents that informed choice is too late. Many thousands of parents throughout the UK are currently struggling to cope with a loved one who has succumbed to a cannabis-induced mental illness. Far too many parents are feeling a sense of despair, hopelessness and bewilderment about who to turn to for help.

I hope to offer these parents some hope by drawing on the experience of hundreds of parents I have come across in my professional career in mental health, and drawing on my own personal experience when my son developed cannabis-induced psychosis.

This book offers some simple tried and tested strategies that parents can use to help to reverse the desperate situation they find themselves in. The book also provides some practical advice on how to communicate and encourage their loved one to seek help and how to deal with the multiple and complex array of agencies that parents have to wrestle with. My book provides QR links to many organisations so that you as the reader will get the best out of this book.

I also hope Gone To Pot will be a wake-up call to the government to proceed with considerable caution with regards to the legalising of cannabis, and not to be pressurised by public and political pressure from some of the large pharmaceutical companies who seek to make huge profits from the sale of legalised cannabis. There is a lot at stake; studies are showing that cannabis is linked to a decline in educational achievement, youngsters dropping out of school, poorer career prospects and unemployment. There is also growing evidence that cannabis could be linked to violence and the increase in knife crime which is all explained later on in the book. There is also increasing evidence that cannabis-induced mental illness is just the tip of the iceberg, that cannabis can have a much subtler impact on people's mental well-being - a loss in personal drive, ambition and disengagement with the rest of society. The research on the subtler effects of cannabis is not as well defined as its link with psychosis, but it is there, as I will point out in this book.

I am concerned that, as a society, we are sleep-walking into legalising cannabis without fully understanding the consequences that legalisation will have on society as a whole. As I will show in the book, I have changed my mind about whether we should legalise cannabis. I have realised that it is not a straightforward 'yes' or 'no' question; there are many other factors to consider before we can begin to even think about legalising cannabis. If we, as a society, do not grasp the very serious issue cannabis poses, then not only will we be condemning tens of thousands of bright young teenagers to a life of isolation, loneliness and despair, we will be placing an enormous burden on parents who will be left to pick up the pieces.

Lastly, the one thing that has kept my interest in mental illness alive is the fact that it is one of the few chronic conditions we can reverse, unlike Parkinson's Disease, Multiple Sclerosis and Alzheimer's. The vast majority of people who experience mental illness get better and go on to live normal lives; even people with chronic conditions such as schizophrenia, can and do improve, and go on to live stable and fulfilling lives. One of the key components to recovery is early intervention and the importance of the family and individual parents. It is often those with loving and supporting parents who have the greatest fighting chance to improve and stabilise their condition. I hope this book will encourage parents to help their children to avoid experimenting with cannabis in the first place and, for those parents already wrestling with cannabis-induced mental illness, I hope this book will provide some positive help during these difficult times.

(Note: I often refer to 'marijuana' instead of cannabis. For the purposes of this book they both mean the same. Marijuana is simply the name other countries, particularly the USA and Australia, use for cannabis.)

PART 1

Chapter 1: The Boy I Used To Know - A Father's Story

Who would have thought such a harmless-looking plant has the ability to profoundly distort people's thoughts, feelings and emotions. The ability to bring about hedonistic bliss and euphoria. The ability to heighten an individual's sense of smell, sound and sight.

In the late 90s, when my son was in his teens, he was seduced by the trappings of this seemingly innocuous plant and ended up with a severe mental illness which affects him to this day.

This chapter graphically recalls those early days of my son's illness, and how we desperately tried to rescue him and find a way out of the nightmare.[2]

A Bolt from the Blue

It was six o'clock on a warm summer's evening when my teenage son asked me a question that was to change my life, and the life of my family forever. I was watching the BBC News; a woman in black was bent over her dead son; she was wailing pitifully. It was all too depressing, so I reached for the remote. As I did so, my 19 year old son, Steve, who had been studying the floor, slowly raised his head and said, "Why did you ring the BBC?" "BBC, Steve, what are you talking about?" "You know!" he snapped back, "Don't deny it, you rung the BBC; they have been talking about me on the television all day." My heart missed a beat; I went cold, I felt sick. All those weeks earlier when I was thinking he might be getting a little depressed because his girlfriend had packed him in and the problems he was

---

[2] Extracts of this chapter originally appeared in a chapter I wrote for Peter Chadwick to include in his book: Schizophrenia: The Positive Perspective. Routledge Taylor & Francis Group, ISBN: 978-0-415-45907-5, 2nd edition. I am very grateful to the publishers for allowing me to use the extracts.

having at college, I was wrong. I knew then I had a very, very sick boy. That day I went to work a dad, and went to bed a carer.

Several excruciating weeks later, Steve was diagnosed with paranoid schizophrenia and hospitalised. My wife and I later discovered that for the previous six months, he had been binging on cannabis, something we had missed. Neither of us had ever smoked or come across cannabis; in fact, I thought he might be suffering with a bit of depression. The psychosis quickly took hold of Steve's mind like some aggressive malignant cancer. We were witnessing the destruction of his mind; it was as if he was trapped in a bottle and drowning in madness. He mumbled in some strange incomprehensible language, walked about the house shouting at the walls, locking himself in his room refusing to come out, and covering his head with the sheets when I walked in. He was a boy gripped by absolute fear and terror. Chris and I helplessly watched on as his beautiful mind was slowly being mutilated. It was more than I could bear at times; it was like watching your son being tortured before your eyes, and there was nothing you could do to stop it. I felt totally powerless. I desperately wanted to reach out and rip out what was destroying his mind. I hoped beyond hope that Steve would wake up and it would all be over, that his mind was clear, and that the cannabis haze had drifted away. Sadly, that was not to be.

The Worst Night of my Life

It was four weeks later during the night of Wednesday 11 August, 1999, when I experienced the worst night of my life. The following day I had an early start, so I went to bed early, I read a few pages of my book, set the alarm and hit the pillow. Three hours later I was awoken by a terrible crash followed by shouting - it was Steve.

I rushed into his bedroom to find him standing in the corner of the room, fear radiating from every pore of his face - his whole body was trembling. "Steve, are you alright, what's the matter?" I asked. Steve just stood transfixed, he seemed paralysed with fear. "Are you my dad?" A quivering voice replied. "Of course I am Steve", I responded. "You're not an alien, are you?" said Steve. "Of course not Steve, it's me, your dad". As I approached him to put my arm around him, he flinched, and backed off. "It's me Steve, it's your dad", trying to reassure him. He turned his face away from me and stared out of the window. He started rambling to himself incoherently. I desperately tried to make out what he was saying but it was impossible. I asked him again if he was alright, but he told me to go away. I asked him if he wanted a drink, but he told me to go back to bed. I asked him to get back into bed which to my surprise he did. As I left the room, I could see the door frame was badly split where it had been violently slammed.

Chris, my wife, was standing in the hallway, her hands clasping her cheeks, I told her that it was perhaps best to leave him and let him go back to sleep. We both got back into bed and lay discussing the situation. Chris was urging me to get Steve into hospital. We had seen his GP four weeks earlier, who had referred Steve to the local Community Mental Health Team. A Psychiatrist had visited Steve and had confirmed that Steve was suffering from psychosis - possibly schizophrenia. We were both in a state of shock. The psychiatrist suggested that we wait to see how things develop, and that they would try and treat his psychosis at home rather than in hospital.

As we lay discussing what to do, there was a sudden almighty crash and the sound of breaking glass - Steve was screaming at the top of his voice -"Fuck off, fuck off, fuck off!" I jumped out of bed and ran to his bedroom. I entered the darkened room, to find Steve silhouetted against the window. He turned and lurched towards me, his six-foot frame stood over me - a beam of light from the hallway draped his face revealing eyes that were full of fear and menace. I was frightened. "It's me Steve, it's your dad". He looked bewildered. "It's alright Steve, it's me", I once again reassured him. He continued to study my face for what seemed ages; he looked totally confused. He suddenly turned away and got back into bed and in a calm voice said, "Go back to bed dad, it's nothing". I went to pick up the pieces of the shattered ashtray, but he angrily told me to get out. I dearly wanted to talk to him; I wanted to find out what I could do to help him, but the truth was I was fearful and uncertain what to do. I returned to our bedroom; Chris was crying. "We have to do something," she sobbed. "He needs to go to hospital now. I want my son back. I want my son back". Steve started shouting again. Chris went to go to him. I told her not to and that we should just wait a while to see if he quietens down, she looked at me and said, "You're frightened, aren't you". Her words were like a spear piercing through me - little Terry Hammond, the poor kid from the back streets of Tooting, the ducker and diver, the born survivor - never lost for a word - knocked for six. Yes, Chris was right - I was frightened. I sat on the edge of the bed feeling defeated. All that so-called experience working in mental health meant nothing. For the first time in my life I simply did know what to do or say - should I cry? Is that what a real man should do? But I don't cry, I have never cried, not once as an adult - not even when my grandfather died, who I was very close to, not even when my beloved Sam the Great Dane had to be put down. Crying - it's a sign of weakness - isn't it?

The sound of Steve continued to dominate the house. I stayed sitting on the edge of the bed, Chris's words still echoing in my head. If I go into his bedroom, would Steve be able to hold himself back this time? Could I defend myself against an attack? He is bigger and far stronger than me; what if he tries to kill me? He is certainly physically capable - who knows what madness lurks inside his head. With a great deal of fear and foreboding, I decided to go to Steve's room, I stood outside for a while, listening. Thankfully, his shouting had abated and he was mumbling away to himself. I opened the door and listened in - he was in bed. I decided that the worst was over and quietly closed the door, relieved that I had not been put to the test. We eventually got Steve into hospital four weeks later - those four weeks were hell!

Several years later, I asked Chris about the night she asked me if I was frightened about going into Steve's bedroom after his shouting. I asked her if she was angry with me and whether she thought I had been a coward. I was somewhat surprised and relieved when she said that she had not been angry with me at all, her anger was with the mental health services for prolonging the dreadful situation we were in, and for allowing Steve to suffer for so long. She did not blame any individual professional; indeed, she thought the psychiatrist had done what he thought was right. It was the endemic failure of the 'mental health system' to react to a crisis that concerned her.

Steve's health continued to decline. He became increasingly paranoid and his behaviour became ever more bizarre and frightening. He made the strangest of wailing noises in the middle of the night and he continued to talk in what seemed like some strange forgotten language. I started to record him and kept a diary of his actions so I could demonstrate to the Mental Health Team how bad things were getting. I used to follow him on his midnight excursion to the local park. I would duck and dive behind trees and bushes like some demented Inspector Clouseau, to see what he was up to, only to discover he was having a quiet fag on the park bench feeding the ducks.

One night, after reading an article about the high risk of suicide amongst newly diagnosed patients, I went into his room to check that he was still breathing. In a panic I started prodding him - Steve woke in a start, "What the fuck you doing Dad?" I felt totally embarrassed, made some excuse and left. Was I becoming a suitable case for treatment?!

Hospitalisation

Steve was finally taken into hospital and there he stayed for three months. When I dropped him off, I felt a great sense of relief as the previous weeks had been a truly dreadful time, but the sense of relief was soon eclipsed by a deep sense of shame. I felt ashamed that I had failed my son. I had let him down. I was abandoning him, at a time when he was in great need. As Steve sat on his hospital bed, passively staring up at the nurse who gently explained the routine, I felt the same sense of anguish I experienced when I left Steve in the hands of his first teacher. He was frightened then, and he was very frightened now. As I gave him a hug and we said our goodbyes, Steve suddenly stood up and said "I don't want to be here dad, I want to come back with you". "You can't, Steve", I replied, struggling for a better response. "But I am feeling alright now," he said, trying to reassure me. I could see Chris welling up. "You can't, Steve, you just can't". Those dreadful nights came flashing through my mind - his constant shouting and screaming at his voices, and having to wash the blood off the walls and carpet where he had been thumping his head against his bedroom wall, regularly apologising to the neighbours for Steve's loud music and swearing in the middle of the night.

"Please Steve, give it a try for Mum's sake." For a few desperate seconds I thought, perhaps, just perhaps, he was OK; maybe this experience had somehow brought him round. I could feel my paternal instincts starting to kick in, my resolve was weakening. The experienced nurse detected that I was struggling, and she was clearly concerned that Chris was getting distressed. "Let your mum and dad get off, Stephen - do you prefer to be called Stephen or Steve?" "Steve," he instinctively replied. "Right, Steve, what do you want for dinner tonight?" she asked, handing him a menu and gently signalling us to leave. I took Chris's hand and left the room and as we did so, Steve called out to us, "You will come tomorrow, won't you?" "Of course, Steve, of course", I reassured him. The corridor leading from the ward to the main entrance was lined with paintings done by patients. I knew it would not be long before Steve's painting would be exhibited - tears poured down my face.

The Long Haul Begins

When Steve emerged from hospital three months later, he was calmer and his paranoia had subsided, but he was a shadow of his former self. He had been put on risperidone, an antipsychotic drug. His vibrancy and natural energy had gone - the fun-loving young man who lived for his mates, football and girls, had become a ghost-like figure. As the weeks and months went by, Steve's strange and bizarre behaviour continued to manifest, as we constantly battled with him to take his medication, which he hated, because he said he felt like a zombie. It was a terrible choice for him. The psychosis seemed to strip him of the basic mores and folk-ways of life; his interaction with people seemed primeval. He avoided all contact. He spent the days pacing around the house, chain-smoking and in an unending dialogue with his voices. At night he sat watching the TV with no sound or wandered around the house. He was oblivious to the disruption he was causing; the trail of coffee stains, the putrid smell of nicotine which permeated around the house, the loud music and his constant manic giggling and laughing. Do we have a zombie son or a psychotic son? What kind of choice is that! At the time we hoped upon hope that Steve would eventually adjust to the side effects of his medication and that his zombie state would subside. We pleaded with him to stick to his medication, and at times demanded that he did. Looking back on it, this was a completely unreasonable demand to make on a young man, but at the time his psychotic state scared us all and I was fearful what might happen to him when he left the house in a psychotic state – it was 'Sophie's choice'.

The Impact on Us

Steve's illness had dramatically changed our lives and the plans we had for our future years. Before Steve's illness, I used to jokingly say to Chris that, when the Saga magazine hits the mat on my fiftieth birthday, we would start to spend on everything that Saga could throw at us. We had more disposable income than we'd ever had in our lives. Our children were carving out their own lives - life was good. Chris and I were really looking forward to being on our own and starting a new phase in our life. But that was not to be. We had become carers, so our plans were on hold for the foreseeable future.

Chris was once asked by a friend what it was like to be a carer. She summed it up well. She said that it was like having a young child again - constantly worrying about him. Worrying when he is asleep, when he is awake and when he is not there; "He's acting different to yesterday; should we tell the doctor?" He has a strange look in his eyes - what does that mean? He is starting to go out in the middle of the night - oh my God, what is he up to?" Chris said that she felt in a state of bereavement because she had lost her son.

In the early years it was hard to leave Steve for any length of time, as we were fearful of what we would find when we got back. He often talked about killing himself; I had visions of finding him dead and then attending his funeral and doing the reading. I would then get a flashing thought that Steve's death may be a happy release from the constant fear and terror he was experiencing day in and day out. Almost immediately I would then start to feel a dreadful guilt for thinking such a terrible thing about my own son.
If people visited the house, Steve would rush to his room as if his life depended on it. It would set off bursts of maniac laughter - it put us on edge all the time people were in the house. One day the plumber came to fix the boiler. Steve suddenly let out an almighty wolf-like cry. "What the bleeding hell was that!" exclaimed the plumber, as he dropped his wrench. "Oh, it's all right; it's my son - he does amateur dramatics, he's rehearsing". The plumber completed his job at breakneck speed and left.

The Effects on my Daughter

I was very conscious that I was not giving Victoria the time she deserved. I was also aware of the pressure Steve was putting on her. Victoria was studying at Southampton University and, as it was only a few miles away; she was still living at home. In the early days when Steve's behaviour was at its most frightening, Victoria often stayed with friends to get some peace. When I was working away, she didn't like leaving her mum alone and slept with her. It was difficult for Victoria when she brought friends back, as Steve's manic laughter could be heard around the house, "Don't worry, that's just my brother", she would say to friends. She likened it to the 'mad' woman in the attic in the novel Jane Eyre.

On one very scary occasion, Steve had taken a dislike to his sister's new boyfriend - as indeed did I. He seemed to dismiss Steve and was not very friendly or kind to him. I got the impression that he thought Steve was just lazy and all he needed was a good kick up the back side. It was a few months into the relationship when, one day, I was talking on the phone, when I suddenly noticed the boyfriend come running full pelt past the window, and then burst through the front door and up the stairs. He was being chased by Steve who had a large lump of wood in his hand. Steve was being chased by my daughter, followed by my wife. It was like a scene out of Keystone Cops. I dropped the phone and leapt up the stairs, past Victoria and my wife, nearly knocking them both through the bannister. I caught up with Steve and the boyfriend who was cowering in the corner of the upstairs landing. As I went to grab the wood from Steve, who was glaring at the boyfriend's reflection in a mirror, he stepped forward and smashed the reflection. He turned to me and calmly said, "He's a bad man, dad", handed me the lump of wood and calmly walked away, leaving everyone in a complete state of shock, not least the boyfriend. I often look back and think how much worse that could have ended up for everyone. A short while later the boyfriend and Victoria went their separate ways - well at least that was a result.

His Non-Compliance

Getting Steve to take his medication and keeping appointments with the support team was a nightmare. For the first couple of years the hospital tried various antipsychotics which Steve would eventually refuse because of their side-effects. While Chris and I fully understood Steve's reasoning, we also had to live with the consequences; his psychosis bursting through and his behaviour and suffering became unbearable. His shouting at his voices in the night, his head-butting of the walls, his nocturnal living. One night I got up and went to Steve and found him sitting on the stairs, his head in his hands. His forehead was covered in blood. I wiped the blood from his forehead. He looked at me and asked where I thought his voices were coming from. I said to him that I thought they were his inner thoughts. He looked at me incredulously and said, "No, that's impossible, it's aliens, I am certain of it".

Self-Neglect

There was a point in Steve's illness when he started to neglect his appearance; he started to look scruffy and dishevelled. He wore the same clothes, his hair was unkempt, and he was unshaven. One day the local policeman called at our house to say that he had received a complaint. My heart sank. Apparently, Steve had pushed a fourteen-year-old boy over a wall. I called Steve to come and talk to the police officer. He told the policemen that the boy was with a gang and they were 'taking the piss' out of him. Steve told the policeman, "I'd had enough, so I walked over to the ringleader and pushed him over the wall; he was lucky I never decked him!" Luckily, I knew the policeman, who was aware of our situation. He gently told Steve not to take the law into his own hands and left - we never heard anymore. The kids kept their distance and Steve got the message to tidy himself up.

The Drinking

Over time Steve started drinking and gradually developed a drinking problem, consuming nine pints a session, four or five days a week, plus an unknown amount from our drinks cabinet. When I challenged him over his drinking, he said that when he got pissed, he felt, 'normal'- he felt like he did when he was a teenager and going out with his mates. Unfortunately, Steve's excursions back to 'normality' caused us untold problems. It put the whole family under even more strain. Apart from the vomit-stained carpets, beer-soaked bed linen and disrupted sleep, his drinking seemed to accentuate his bizarre behaviour and reduce his inhibitions.

Thankfully, Steve was never aggressive or violent to us, but the disruption and the anguish that followed took its toll. Chris could not hold her anger with Steve; she would demand that, if he did not stop drinking, he would have to leave the house, which I argued against. But Chris was right, his behaviour was unacceptable as it threatened to undo all the work that everyone had put into Steve. Let alone the anguish he was causing. Chris's outbursts definitely had an impact on him, especially when one day she burst into tears in front of him, in total despair. Eventually we made a 'contract' with Steve to get him to limit his drinking, which he did try to maintain, and slowly he did cut down. It took time and patience, several months - well, years to be honest - but we got there. Steve still has the occasional excursion back to 'normality', but then who wouldn't?

A Beacon of Hope

It was two years into his illness when we were at one of our regular review meetings at the hospital between the psychiatrist, Steve, my wife and me. The psychiatrist asked Steve about his voices and where he thought they came from. Steve said he thought aliens were trying to communicate with him. The doctor then asked him how certain he was of that. Steve thought for a moment and then replied "90% certain". Then the psychiatrist asked what I thought was a brilliant question. "So, Steve, what's the 10%?" Steve pondered for a moment and replied, "Good question; I suppose they could be in my head". The psychiatrist gave a reassuring smile and nodded. Christine looked at me, a tear rolling down her face and we both smiled, Steve's ten percent uncertainty was our beacon of hope.

Some years later, after a long period of therapy which I will discuss later, the same psychiatrist asked Steve if he still heard voices. "Yes, of course I do", Steve responded. The doctor then asked that crucial question: "Where do you think they come from Steve". Steve thought for a moment and replied, "In my head". Brilliant, I thought, fantastic! But then the psychiatrist went on and asked him the same follow up question as he did before: "How certain are you, Steve, that your voices are coming from your head?" Steve pondered for a moment and said, "88% certain". "So, what's the 12% doubt then, Steve?" the psychiatrist replied. Steve thought for a moment and said, "Well, it's the things my voices say. I don't think I could be that clever." My eyes welled up as I realised then just how low Steve's self-esteem was. It dawned on me that we still had a long way to go, but at least we were going in the right direction.

When he was more settled and on regular medication, he often asked me to stay with him; unfortunately, this was often late at night. He just wanted me to watch the TV with him or listen to music. I was always mindful of increasing that ten percent beacon of hope. Sometimes he was happy for me just to sit in the room in silence - I think my presence helped him overcome the fear he was clearly experiencing. The problem for me was the lack of sleep was causing me problems at work as, on more than one occasion, I fell asleep at my desk. Occasionally, I disappeared into the toilet so I could grab a few minutes' sleep. One day I fell into a deep sleep sitting on the loo, and was woken up an hour later by a colleague knocking on the door to see if I was OK. Thankfully they all knew my situation and gave me a lot of support, including my boss, Paul Farmer CBE, who went on to become the Chief Executive Officer of the national mental health charity MIND.

The one thing that did seem to relax Steve in those early days was car rides. Very often I would get home from work and, the minute I was through the door, Steve would ask me to take him out, "Dad, I could really do with going out in the car, my voices have been really bad today". How could I refuse? We would go out for an hour or so and always the same route. Mostly we sat in silence. For Steve it was a distraction from spending hour upon hour being plagued by voices which I guess he was still trying to figure out.

It was a constant juggling act between supporting Steve, finishing that important report from work, and spending time with Chris and my daughter Victoria.

As time passed, Steve did start to slowly improve and our life began to stabilise; this was mostly down to getting the right medication, CBT (Cognitive Behavioural Therapy), and input from the community support workers who helped Steve to get out of the house, and eventually got him to attend a day centre, which proved vital. I will go into much more detail in Chapters 7 and 8 about the actions parents can take to help their loved ones to regain stability, and for the family to regain some sense of normality into their lives.

20 Years on

It has been over twenty years since Steve was in hospital. He still hears his voices, he still gets paranoid, and is perpetually plagued by anxiety and indecision. Steve does not work and has no real close friends other than his family whom he very much depends on. But the difference between those early scary years and now is that Steve is in greater control of his psychosis. I asked him recently whether his voices were as bad as they were ten years ago. His reply shocked me: "My voices are as much with me now as the first day I heard them," he replied. "Really, Steve?" I replied. "You surprise me as you seem so much more in control these days." "I am," he replied. "It's just that the voices are no longer centre-stage, they are out there in the wings; they still jabber away, but I have learnt to ignore them. It's only when I get stressed that they come centre-stage and really annoy me."

Steve attends an animal charity three days a week run by a local charity called Phoenix. He gets a great deal out of going as do the other people who attend. As Steve says to our friends, "I go to work three days a week and I work on the land." Being able to say he 'goes to work' is crucial for Steve's self-esteem, as it is for his colleagues. It's a real joy to watch them going about their tasks, supporting each other, each normalised by their toil. Seeing this always brings a warm smile to my face.

Sadly, Phoenix, like so many charities doing such essential work, live from hand to mouth. They don't get direct grants from the state anymore; the previous horticultural project Steve attended had to shut down because of funding issues. The fact that such projects still have to rely on Victorian philanthropy in the fifth richest country in the world, goes beyond belief.

The benefits of supported employment to society are immeasurable. Apart from giving us carers an essential break and providing structure to the lives of their loved ones, they save the tax-payer millions of pounds every year. The South London Maudsley NHS Trust reported to the National Audit Committee recently that the cost of a hospital admission is over £3,000 a week, or £39k for a three-month stay (the same period my son was in hospital). So, the cost of keeping just one person in hospital for three months would enable many sheltered workplaces to function for a full year, supporting 15 or more clients. Yet many such charities have little or no grants and have to live from hand to mouth, relying on a local church and staff to do car boot sales to survive. It's an absolute public disgrace that we treat essential services in this way.

Since austerity policies were introduced in the UK in 2010, thousands of community care programmes supporting some of the country's most vulnerable citizens have been forced to close because of loss of funding, leaving many former clients, who do not have close family, living lonely and isolated lives. It's therefore not surprising that suicide and homelessness amongst people with mental illness is on the increase according to the Samaritans and 'The Big Issue'. To compound this, thousands of mental health hospital beds have closed. The Chairperson of the Royal College of Psychiatrists, Professor Wendy Burn has stated:

> **"Trusts struggling with dangerously high levels of bed occupancy are being forced to send seriously ill people hundreds of miles away from their homes for care. That must stop."**[3]

To pour petrol on a burning fire, the government's changes to the benefits system have left thousands of people with severe mental illness in abject poverty. Thankfully, Steve has friends and family around him to champion his cause and to protect him from the clumsy and thoughtless decisions of misguided politicians and policy-makers.

Now I have got that off my chest, let me get back to Steve. When Steve is not volunteering for Phoenix, he tends to keep himself to himself. Steve mostly tries to avoid engaging with people because of his voices and acute anxiety. He does respond politely when he is approached but will withdraw as soon as he can to the sanctuary of his mind.

I often think if Steve had been alive during the First World War he would have been constantly receiving 'White Feathers' (the sign of cowardice given out to men who did not go to war). For all intents and purposes Steve looks a big strong strapping man, but of course he is just as disabled as if he had an arm blown off, or his legs shattered. Losing the ability to control your own thoughts, your feelings, and having your mind constantly playing tricks with you, is equally disabling as other life-changing physical disabilities. Very recently Steve told me that when someone talks to him, he cannot always tell whether it's the person's words he is hearing or his own voices. He said that's why he laughs sometimes when people talk to him. I can't begin to know how I would cope with such a disability.

Steve is a hero as far as I am concerned, as are the thousands of others who have to cope with such disabilities. They all deserve the very highest respect and admiration for what they endure - not rejection, not prejudice and not discrimination. Above all, people with such highly disabling conditions, such as schizophrenia, deserve kindness, care and support from the state. Closing thousands of day centres, sheltered workshops and social support schemes, and making them do double somersaults to get their benefits, is cruel and shows gross neglect to some of our most vulnerable citizens.

The Future

The dark days of Steve head-butting the wall are over. He is in much more control of his psychosis. He still talks to his voices and gets anxious and paranoid at times, but he understands that it's 'faulty wiring in his brain', not aliens. He knows his limitations and, although he hates being like it, he has learnt to live with it, and makes the best of his life that he can. Chris and I can now go on holiday and not be constantly worrying about Steve - a quick phone call each day reassures him and us. Our very supportive daughter and son-in-law have produced two lovely grandchildren, so Steve is surrounded by stability, normality and love. (Steve, lives in a small annex adjoining our house where he lives reasonably independently).

Steve is now 42 and is going to require some help and support for a few years to come, but I do believe he has reached the point that will ensure he does not easily slip back into a relapse. He reads his mind well and knows how to reduce and avoid stress, which remains the last big challenge to overcome.

It was the first few years that were the worst because it felt like we had all been dropped into the middle of a dark and dangerous forest without any knowledge of where we were, which direction to go, or where to get help - it was a grim time. But help did come, and slowly we were able to see a glimmer of light which gave us the hope that we needed. Life does get better.

So when I look back at that day I watched that poor woman in black on TV grieving over her dead son, all those years ago, I often think she will never be able to feel the warmth of her son's body again, never be able to hug him, never smile with him again. At least I can still hug Steve and enjoy a pint down the pub with him - which we do.

PART 2

Chapter 2: Understanding Cannabis

The Clue is in its Biological Make-Up

When I emerged from the dark days of Steve's illness, I decided to try and understand more about cannabis, I was curious how such a harmless-looking plant could trigger such a reaction. It was not until I delved into the biology of the plant that I was able to grasp why such an innocent-looking plant could cause so much unhappiness.

I soon discovered that cannabis is in fact, a highly complex plant, being made up of 400 chemicals. The two main elements of cannabis are THC (delta-9-tetrahydrocannabinol) and CBD (cannabidiol[4]). The THC causes the psychoactive reaction to the brain, disrupting and distorting thought processing. It is the THC that gives users the sense of being 'high', euphoric, relaxed and having heightened senses such as smell, colour and sound. However, for some, THC can cause paranoia, lethargy and anxiety. It can also affect concentration and coordination, which is why it can be dangerous to drive and use mechanical equipment. THC is a very powerful substance and cannabis is thought to be the only plant in the world that produces such a toxic substance[5]. It is believed that it acts as a defence mechanism for the plant.

The second key element is CBD, which is associated with a wide range of medical benefits, including pain relief, nausea, treatment of cancer, glaucoma, HIV, symptoms of post-traumatic stress and many more. As we will discover later, some of these claims have been ratified by scientists, but many more have not. One of the

---

[4] Cannabis, a complex plant: Different compounds & different effects on individuals: Zerrin Attakan Ther. Adv Psychopharmacol, 2012 Dec 2
[5] Nature Out Look: The Bioengineering of Cannabis, 28 Aug 2019

fascinating properties of CBD is that it is thought to have antipsychotic properties, which actually counterbalance the psychotic part of the plant (THC).So we have a plant which can produce psychoactive reactions in the brain and cause people to lose control of their thinking process and, at the same time, produce a chemical compound that counters the psychoactive reaction produced by the THC. (This perhaps helps to explain why some people say smoking cannabis can help their psychosis.)

A Quick History of Cannabis

Human use of cannabis goes back thousands of years and it is one of the earliest known plants to be cultivated. Cannabis has been used for food, medicine, rope-making, religious ceremonies and for recreational purposes. In first century China, scholars recorded in the first comprehensive reference guide on herbs and drugs called the Pen-ts'ao ching, that excessive cannabis smoking caused 'seeing the Devil'. By 100 AD, Chinese physicians believed the drug, if taken in excess, will make one communicate with the spirits and lightens one's body'[6].

During Napoleon Bonaparte's invasion of Egypt in 1798, alcohol was not available as Egypt was an Islamic country. In place of alcohol, Bonaparte's troops resorted to trying hashish (extracts from the cannabis plant) which they found to their liking. As a result of the conspicuous consumption of hashish by the troops, the smoking of hashish and consumption of drinks containing the substance, it was banned in October 1800 because of the adverse effects it was having on his troops and the local people[7]. In 1904, Dr. George F. W. Ewens, the Superintendent of the Punjab Lunatic Asylum, produced a report 'Insanity Following the Use of Indian Hemp' (an extract of cannabis). His report states:

---

[6] http://dx.doi.org/10.1590/S1516-44462006000200015 (accessed 21.7.20)
[7] https://en.wikipedia.org/wiki/Cannabis_in_Egypt (cannabis: A History by Martin Booth pp76-77 ISBN 978-1-250-08219-0) (Accessed 2/9/21)

> There is a special form of mental disease met with-in India, usually classed as Toxic Insanity which seems to have direct relation to the excessive use of hemp drugs. The symptoms are entirely mental, among the large number I have now seen, unlike the results of alcohol[8].

During the 1920s the Egyptian government was so concerned about the detrimental effects cannabis was having on the working population, it requested that cannabis be added to the 'Geneva International Convention on Narcotics Control'. In the UK on 28 September 1925, the Dangerous Drug Act became law and cannabis was included in the list of 'dangerous' drugs and was made an illegal substance. Many countries followed suit and, by the end of the twentieth century, most developed countries had banned cannabis use.

During the early part of the 1900s, cannabis use was mostly by the middle classes; very few 'working class' used it. That changed in the 60s with the growth of the flower power movement and the Vietnam war, when many young, working-class soldiers started using it to relieve the stress of war, and carried on using it on their return.

Cannabis use quickly spread to Europe and increased in popularity. By the turn of the millennium cannabis became the most used illicit drug in Europe with an estimated 23 million 15 to 64 year olds having used the drug in the past year and about 12 million 15 to 64 year olds in the last month. The UK was amongst the highest users in Europe; according to the United Nations Office of Drugs and Crime[9], 5.8 million UK adults (1 in 10) had used cannabis in the last year. The situation was worst for young people; a UK Government survey in 2000 revealed that 44% of 16 to 29 year olds

---

[8] https://pdfs.semanticscholar.org/9582/621e07e54b9025539d3b70f1d1e46f079024.pdf (accessed: 18:06.20)
[9] https://www.tni.org/es/node/17047 (assessed 2/9/21)

had used cannabis at some time in their lives, 22% had done so in the last year, and 14% in the previous month[10]. The use of cannabis in the UK has thankfully declined (see Figure 1 below)[11] from the 'heady' days of the 90s/2000, although cannabis use does appear to be on the increase once again.

Figure 1: Reported Proportion of Adults Using Cannabis, 1996-2018, Age Groups 16-24 & 16-59

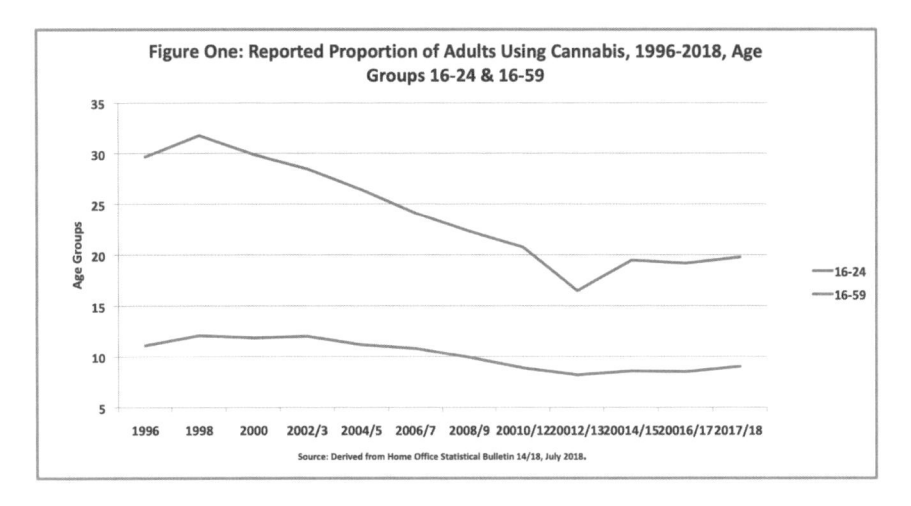

Home Office statistical bulletin July 2018

Cannabis as a Medicine

The medical use of cannabis also goes back centuries. In ancient China physicians mixed cannabis into medicine to treat pain and used it as an anaesthetic. In Ancient Greece cannabis was used to stop nose bleeds. Queen Victoria is alleged to have used it for period pains. The use of cannabis as a medicine increased during the 1900s and its use continues to increase. Prior to the second world war there were 2,000 cannabis medicines produced by over

280 manufacturers (BBC Panorama, 2001[12]). Whilst these products were produced without any scientific basis, there was considerable anecdotal evidence that cannabis-based medicines had some impact on alleviating certain conditions, particularly pain relief. As modern medicines developed during the 1900s, new and more laboratory-tested drugs were developed such as aspirin (1899), and cannabis medicines fell out of favour as people turned towards the more scientifically proven drugs. The use of cannabis as a medicine continued but was very much a niche market.

In 1973 Tod H Mikuya, a psychiatrist from California, published a paper claiming that cannabis helped glaucoma[13]. There were further studies undertaken, most of them small scale, highlighting the potential therapeutic benefits of cannabis for a variety of medical conditions, such as pain relief, help with muscle spasms, and relief from the nausea caused by chemotherapy. This helped to spark a renewed public interest in cannabis. Medicalised cannabis provided a strong argument for those who for years had been campaigning to legalise cannabis, claiming it was a harmless recreational drug and, far from being dangerous, actually had healing qualities. As the use of cannabis increased during the 1960s, so did the calls to legalise it. Pressure groups sprang up calling for the decriminalisation of cannabis, riding on the back of its therapeutic value for a range of medical conditions.

Can you Become Addicted to Cannabis?

The answer is yes, according to the National Institute on Drugs in the US. Marijuana (the American word for cannabis) use can lead to 'marijuana use disorder', which takes the form of addiction in severe cases. Recent data suggests that 30% of those who use marijuana may have some degree of marijuana - use disorder.

---

12 http://news.bbc.co.uk/1/hi/programmes/panorama/4104744.stm (accessed: 30.06.20)
13 Mikuma, T.H., (1973) Marijuana Medical Papers, 1839-72. Medical-Comp Press

People who begin using marijuana before the age of 18 are four to seven times more likely to develop a marijuana - use disorder than adults". The UK Government's own website FRANK states:

Heavy cannabis users often get cravings and find it hard not to take the drug – even when they know it's causing them physical, mental or social problems.

When heavy users do try to stop, they can:
- **feel moody and irritable**
- **feel sick**
- **find it hard to sleep**
- **find it hard to eat**
- **experience sweating and shaking**
- **get diarrhoea**

If you roll your spliffs (a term often used to describe mixing cannabis with tobacco), you're also at risk of getting addicted (or staying addicted) to nicotine. A World Health Organisation (WHO) report talks about cannabis users becoming dependent on cannabis: (Chapter 9.1.4 **'What we know about the long-term effects of regular cannabis use'**). The report also states that 'Regular cannabis users can develop dependence on the drug. The risk may be around 1 in 10 among those who ever use cannabis, 1 in 6 among adolescent users, and 1 in 3 among daily users'.

A point of clarification: you will often read of people becoming 'addicted' as opposed to being 'dependent'. Very briefly, addiction happens when there are biochemical changes to the brain which makes the individual reliant on a substance. That is why it is often referred to as a 'disease' because of biochemical changes to the brain. This happens most notably to excessive drinkers who go on to develop alcoholism. Heavy use of cannabis can cause similar changes to the brain.

Dependency is more of a 'physical desire' for cannabis and, although you will get a very strong urge to use it, it would be easier for you to stop because your brain has not gone through a biochemical change. Dependence is very often a stage before addiction. That is why it is essential that, when someone develops cannabis-induced psychosis, it is crucial that their dependence or addiction is also treated. If you would like to know more on this subject then either contact your GP or local Community Mental Health Team. Also, you could talk to one of the specialist mental health charities which specialise in drug misuse; charities such as:
Adfam: 02038179410, www.adfam.org.uk
Families Anonymous: 02074984680, www.famanon.org.uk
DrugFam: 03008883853, www.drugfam.co.uk

Is Cannabis a 'Gateway' to Hard Drugs such as Heroin?

This is not a straightforward question because there is no evidence, as far as I can find, that using cannabis will cause a person to use class 'A' drugs or 'hard drugs' such as heroin, cocaine or amphetamines. But then there is no evidence to say that it doesn't lead to class 'A' drugs either.

It is correct to say that the vast majority of the 2.6 million cannabis users[14] do not go on to use hard drugs. Supporters of cannabis quite rightly argue that cannabis users also smoke tobacco and drink alcohol, so you cannot just point the finger at cannabis. However, a study done in the US in 2015 has focused upon the gateway between cannabis and other, harder, illegal drugs[15]. The study found that 44.7% of regular cannabis users (weekly and daily) went on

---

14 Home Office Drug Misuse: Findings from the 2018/9 Crime Survey for England and Wales
15 Secades-Villa, R. (et.al) (2014) Probability and predictors of the cannabis gateway effect: A national study. Found at: https://www.ncbi.nlm.nih.gov/pmc/articles/PMC4291295/ (accessed: 29.06.20)

to use hard drugs. That still does not prove that cannabis 'causes' a person to use them, but it does show that it substantially increases the risk, especially if they are regular users of cannabis.

I fully accept that it is only a minority of users of cannabis who will go on to use hard drugs, but it is not a small proportion of **heavy** users of cannabis, as the research shows, and remember we are often talking about young vulnerable teenage kids, young people who lack maturity and can easily be led.

There are very good reasons why cannabis users graduate to hard drugs; these include:

- Accessing cannabis can bring them in contact with members of criminal gangs, especially if they are a regular client.
- Cannabis users may look for a bigger 'high'
- Associating with peers who are prepared to break the law
- Living in a run-down area
- Poor parental supervision
- Childhood trauma
- Coming out of care and having no family support or friends
- Poverty and homelessness
- A lack of self-worth and feeling detached from society.

In my professional career, and in my personal life, I have seen for myself cannabis users graduating to hard drugs. It is true that most did not, but a large minority did. One of my closest friend's teenage child started smoking cannabis at the age of 14, graduated to hard drugs in adulthood, and has become continually hooked on them ever since. Now in their 40s, their child's life is a complete mess and the parents are in perpetual despair. Sadly, this story could be told by thousands of parents up and down the country.

Is it Better to Vape or Smoke Synthetic Cannabis (Cannabinoids)?

I am afraid it makes no difference; in fact, it could be worse. Vaping may reduce the impact on your physical health as it may do for tobacco smokers but, if the THC levels are high, then so is the risk to your mental health. According to https://www.drugrehab.com (accessed: 29.06.20) vaping could cause more harm because vaping could lead to inhaling even higher levels of THC than smoking cannabis. This is particularly worrying as trends in the US show that vaping is becoming more popular than smoking amongst teenagers[16].

Synthetic cannabis, or Cannabinoids as it is known, could be even more dangerous. The UK government's 'FRANK' website states:

> **The risks of synthetic cannabinoids are similar to natural cannabis, but because synthetic cannabinoids are more potent, it is easy to use too much and experience the unpleasant and harmful effects. This higher potency also means that the effects may last for longer. Also, because many synthetic cannabinoids are new, they may have unknown effects too[17].**

Recent Moves to Decriminalise Cannabis

Holland was, in modern times, the first country in Europe to start relaxing the laws on cannabis. In 1976 they passed a law permitting low-level possession, although it was still illegal to consume in public. Prosecutors and the police adopted a 'tolerance' attitude

---

[16] National Institute on Drugs Abuse – Monitoring The Future Survey: High School and Youth Trends Drug Facts: accessed 12. 11.20
[17] https://www.talktofrank.com/drug/synthetic-cannabinoids (accessed: 29.06.20)

to cannabis use, which led to the creation of the famous 'Coffee Shops' where you could purchase and smoke cannabis without fear of prosecution. In 2001 Luxembourg became the first European country to actually de-criminalise cannabis, which meant that users would only get a fine for a first offence as opposed to a custodial sentence. In 2013 Uruguay became the first country to fully legalise cannabis for recreational use followed by several other countries, including Georgia, Canada, eleven states in the USA and the capital city of Australia, Canberra.

Cannabis-Induced Mental Illness Starts to Increase

The increased use of cannabis during the 1970s and 80s coincided with an increase in the numbers of young teenagers being admitted to hospital with cannabis-induced psychosis. Studies in America, Australia and Europe showed alarming levels of psychosis amongst young people. One of the most important studies was undertaken in Sweden in 1987 by Andreason, Engstrom, Allebeck, and Rydberg.[18] They followed 45,750 young men who had confirmed they had used cannabis more than 50 times. The results of the study found that these men were six times more likely to experience schizophrenia than those who had never used cannabis.

Alarm Raised by Mental Health Staff and Parents

It was not just the scientific research that was exposing the dangers of cannabis, but the huge number of health professionals working on the front line. They could see first-hand the impact cannabis was having on young people, especially in the large cities. A number of mental health charities also started to warn of the dangers of cannabis. The national UK charity, Rethink Mental Illness (www.rethink.org.uk), which represents thousands of parents,

[18] Andreasson,S.,Engström,A.,Allebeck,P.,Rydberg.,(1987) "Cannabis and Schizophrenia: A Longitudinal Study of Swedish Conscripts" The Lancet. Vol.330. Issue 8574, 26.12.87.

began receiving calls from its members expressing alarm about the impact cannabis was having on family members. An example of one Rethink member's experience:

> **"My daughter started taking cannabis at college and within a few months it made her completely psychotic, she lost her place at college her friends her part time job and her flat. Her life has spiralled out of control."**

In the late 1990s, I was working for Rethink Mental Illness and persuaded my colleagues to do a campaign on cannabis use to see how widespread the problem really was. During the time I was researching the issue, unbeknown to me and my wife, my son Steve had already started to experiment with it with his mates. Ironically, it was in the middle of my research into the dangers of cannabis that my son developed cannabis-induced psychosis. By 2004 my anger and determination to expose the dangers of cannabis had grown with a vengeance. I agreed with my boss at Rethink to tell my own story to the media, with the consent of my son. So, we sent out a number of press releases. *The Times*[19] was quick to seize on it and ran with the story. It became a national story and was soon picked up by other media outlets. Many more parents started to come forward expressing alarm at what cannabis was doing to their loved ones. It soon became clear that cannabis was indeed a very big issue and one that was having a very serious impact on the lives of thousands of parents up and down the country.

During the 2000s, I contributed to numerous media articles and took part in various television programmes. I was also invited to contribute to academic books and articles. My son's story was featured on Panorama[20], Newsnight and many more. My son and I agreed to take part in a programme looking at 'comp genes' which

---

19 Boggan.S.,"If cannabis is safe why am I psychotic? The Times 07.01.04
20 http://news.bbc.co.uk/1/hi/programmes/panorama/4104744.stm 19.06.05

scientists believed were linked to cannabis-induced psychosis; sure enough; Steve's genes showed a link. The Mental Health charity, SANE, also raised concerns and campaigned on the dangers of cannabis. Marjorie Wallace, the founder of SANE and Chief Executive, is a passionate campaigner. We have both appeared on the radio together warning the public of its dangers.

A False Dawn

During the early 2000s the cannabis story continued to develop as more and more countries around the world were expressing alarm about the impact cannabis was having on increasing numbers of young people. At the time, along with my colleagues at Rethink Mental Illness, I was feeling optimistic; after five years of heavy campaigning it seemed that the message was finally getting across. Sadly, this was naive thinking, as we had underestimated the determination of the cannabis supporters who still vehemently contested what we considered was overwhelming evidence that cannabis was linked to schizophrenia. They claimed the studies were flawed. They also claimed that the increase in admissions to mental health units was not down to cannabis, but other social factors. They argued that alcohol was far more dangerous than cannabis.

It became clear to us that cannabis was becoming a casualty of the wider debate on drugs, as governments were looking at ways of dealing with the huge illegal trade, costing billions of pounds. In the UK the National Crime Agency estimated the cost of illegal drugs to the UK economy to be over £10 billion annually if you include the cost of treating drug addiction, the associated crime, including violence and stealing, and the huge cost to the criminal justice system.

UK Temporarily Decriminalises Cannabis

Even the UK Government succumbed to the pressure when, in 2004, the then Home Secretary, David Blunkett, downgraded cannabis from a class 'B' to a class 'C' drug, which is considered less harmful by Parliament. However, those of us who had lobbied so hard were not prepared to sit back and watch the government undo all our hard work. Rethink Mental Illness lobbied the government and, as a senior manager with the cannabis brief, I met with the then new Minister, Carolyn Flint, along with my Rethink colleagues. Our argument was simple: decriminalising cannabis sent completely the wrong message to young people, who were the ones most at risk of developing cannabis-induced psychosis. Decriminalisation would be saying to young people that cannabis is OK to smoke.

It was clear that the UK Government, and other governments around the world, who were relaxing the laws on cannabis, were way behind the curve. The cannabis that was flooding the streets was far more potent than the cannabis of the 60s; its biological make-up had been genetically modified by organised crime in order to increase the levels of THC and reduce the CBD to give cannabis a greater 'kick', which was proving to be devastating to many teenagers. In the 1960s the THC levels were around 3 to 5%. Today the average level in the UK is more than 15%[21]. In Holland you can buy cannabis with 67% THC[22]. Finnish research has shown that a young teenager using cannabis just five times or more could develop psychosis[23]. So, just think, an innocent young vulnerable teenager could go off to Amsterdam with his mates for a fun weekend, smoke 5 high potency joints and return with potentially serious brain damage.

21 Jamapysychiatry.com – Will Legalisation and Comercialisation of Cannabis Use Increase the Incidence and Prevalence of Psychosis? Murray & Hall
22 The Lancet: The Contribution of Cannabis Use to Variations in the Incidences of Psychosis Disorders Across Europe
23 Adolescent Cannabis Use, Baseline Prodromal Symptoms and the risk of Psychosis – British Journal of Psychiatry April 2018

The seriousness of the situation with cannabis did start to get across and to its credit, in 2008 the UK Government under Gordon Brown reversed the decision to downgrade cannabis and put it back to a class 'B'. This fired up the supporters of cannabis who, once again, attempted to debunk the evidence and push for legalisation. They focused on the therapeutic and medical value of cannabis created by the CBD. They had some powerful backers - multinational corporations who latched on to the potential huge profits of a legalised cannabis market. The American broadcaster CNBC reported in May 2019 that, if cannabis were legalised, then the market could be worth $44 billion by 2028[24]. In 2018, London hosted its first ever 'Cannabis Invest Conference'[25].

A large number of big corporations have become big proponents for legalising cannabis; they see huge profits to be made, and governments see their share through taxes. That is why large corporations are now spending millions on marketing cannabis as well as lobbying politicians to decriminalise it. (I will expand on this later in the book.)

The Confusing Messages to the Public

For members of the public trying to get their heads around the cannabis debate, it has become incredibly confusing. On the one hand, increasing numbers of scientific studies are showing a definite link between cannabis and mental illness and, on the other hand, similar studies are showing that cannabis has medicinal benefits. More recently the message has been even more confusing to the public with many countries around the world deregulating cannabis, including Portugal, Australia, Canada, the US and many others. In 2018 the UK allowed cannabis to be used for medical use and the demand to deregulate it for recreational use is growing. During the 2019 UK election, the Lib Dems, under their leader, Jo Swinson, stated that she had taken cannabis and liked it. She pledged to decriminalise cannabis if they were in power, emphasising that cannabis could be worth £1.5 billion per year in tax revenue. Public opinion is shifting and increasing numbers of people consider cannabis should be legalised. In a poll in *The Independent*, fifty-nine percent said they thought cannabis should be legalised [26]. But would fifty-nine percent still be keen if they knew some of the more ominous facts?

Chapter 3 - The Link Between Cannabis and Mental Illness

To understand the link between cannabis and mental illness, it is important to understand the causes of mental illness. In this Chapter we will explore the many factors that can lead to mental illness and the science behind the link with cannabis.

Understanding Mental Health

Our mental health is how people see us and how we see ourselves, our personality, thoughts, feelings and our behaviour. Good mental health is a state of well-being when you and others consider that you are in control of your thoughts, feelings and behaviour. The World Health Organisation (WHO) defines mental health as:

> **A state of well-being in which the person realises his or her own attitudes, can cope with normal stresses of life, can work productively and fruitfully and is able to make a contribution to his or her community** [27].

Most of us have periods in our life when we experience some form of mental health issue, in the same way that we all experience physical ill health issues - diseases, broken limbs, sports injury, colds, aches and pains. Our mental health is no different; we can all feel mentally vulnerable at times - the first day at school, exams, the breakup of a relationship, sleepless nights, worrying about work. How often do we lie in bed tossing and turning thinking about some mini-crisis, not able to shift the worry out of our heads, but when we wake up in the morning the crisis seems less acute. In the cold light of day, we have been able to rationalise the problem and get a perspective on it.

---

[27] World Health Organization. (2004) Promoting Mental Health. Concepts, Emerging Evidence, Practice. Geneva: WHO.

It is normal to experience worry and anxiety; in fact our survival depends on it. Being anxious and worrying helps us to avoid exposing ourselves to dangerous situations; driving too fast, going close to the edge of a cliff, being wary of dangerous animals and getting anxious about our children's safety. If we had not been 'wired up' to become anxious, then our ancestors may well have been eaten by sabre-tooth tigers millions of years ago.

It is also important to feel unhappy and sad; without it we would not care when someone dies, or when someone close to us was ill or in need of help. Being able to empathise and relate to other people's sadness and pain - having the empathy to be compassionate and kind is what sets us apart from most other creatures. Without the ability to empathise and be compassionate our species would be in a constant state of anger, rage and violence. So, in the right circumstances, sadness and worry, especially about other people, is a welcome emotion and one we must learn to accept and trust.

The difference in someone with a mental illness, is when the sadness, anxiety or worry is prolonged. When their thoughts and feelings become exaggerated and last for days and even weeks. When anxiety starts to dominate a person's life and the lives of those close to them. That is when the individual may not be coping and may need some help to stabilise their unwelcome thoughts, feelings and behaviour.

There are many types of mental illnesses the most common and well known are: Anxiety, Stress, Panic Disorders, Depression, Bipolar, Psychosis and Schizophrenia. Other conditions include; Eating disorders, Phobias, Personality Disorder, Autism, Alzheimer's disease. Many, many more have been highlighted by

NHS Information, Scotland[28].

As a species we still have a long way to go before we evolve to the point that mental illness no longer affects us. We have reached a point in evolution that according to the World Health Organisation, around one in four of us will be treated for mental illness at some time in our lives; that's over 16 million people in the UK - nearly twice the size of London's population.

Another way of looking at it is the next time you see children playing in a school playground: for every 100 children happily running around, 25 of those children will go on to be treated for a mental illness - depression, anxiety, bipolar or eating disorder. One child will develop schizophrenia and worryingly, according to the Mental Health Foundation, 10 of those 100 children will already be showing symptoms of mental health issues[29].

The causes of mental illness are complex and wide-ranging. Mental illness can exist in the genes we inherit, the society we live in, and the way we live our lives. It is important to stress that the vast majority of people who experience mental illness do recover and are able to carry on with their lives - early intervention is key, something I will talk about later in the book.

The Role our Genes Play

Human beings are made up of around 24,000 genes. Each parent passes on a set of genes to their children. Some genes passed on can mutate which can make the individual more prone to a particular disease. This is often referred to as having a 'predisposition' or a 'susceptibility' to a certain condition. Parents with a history of heart disease, for example, are more likely to inherit the condition and pass it on to future generations than a

28 https://www.nhsinform.scot/illnesses-and-conditions/mental-health (accessed: 19.06.20)
29 https://www.mentalhealth.org.uk/a-to-z/c/children-and-young-people (accessed: 19.06.20)

family with no history of heart disease. Huntington's Disease is perhaps the most extreme example. A mother or a father carrying the Huntington's disease gene has a 50% chance of passing it on to one of their children[30].

Mental illness is also a condition that can be carried on through the family genes. Rethink has identified schizophrenia as a clear example: if your mother has the condition, the risk of you developing schizophrenia increases to around 13%. If you are one of identical twins with schizophrenia, then your chances increase to over 45%[31].

It is important to stress that, even if you have inherited genes from your parents that give you a predisposition to mental illness, it does not mean that you will develop the condition. Your genes only increase the risk. You could be born with a predisposition to mental illness and live a life free from any condition. On the other hand, you could be born with a low predisposition to mental illness, but still develop mental health issues because you have been exposed to a particular social trauma or life event.

Social Factors

Over many years, studies have shown that social and environmental factors can play a major role in triggering mental illness (World Mental Health Organisation - Social Determinate of Mental Illness). Child abuse is an obvious example. Other factors include poor physical health, stress at work, relationship problems, debt, poverty, poor housing and loneliness. Personal traumas such as a bereavement, a serious accident, or being exposed to war can all play a major role. Think of all the young men who joined the

---

30 https://www.empr.com/home/tools/patient-fact-sheets/huntingtons-disease-patient-information-fact-sheet (accessed:19.06.20)
31 https://www.rethink.org/advice-and-information/carers-hub/does-mental-illness-run-in-families/ (assessed 2/9/21)

forces, mental illness-free, who were exposed to a war zone, and then went on to develop post-traumatic stress, something we now have a better understanding of. The thought that many of these poor men were shot or seen as cowards in the First World War still haunts us all.

Lifestyle and Personal Choices

Lifestyle and personal choices can very much determine our mental health and well-being. Research in Germany[32] has shown that a healthy lifestyle can reduce the risk of poor mental health and improve our overall well-being. This requires keeping physically fit, maintaining a healthy weight and moderate drinking. The job you choose can also have a major impact. Studies have identified that teachers and health and social care workers experience higher than average mental health problems – often due to workload, poor support and direction from managers[33]. The building trade is also prone to higher levels of mental health and, sadly, suicide. Often workers have to work away from home and drinking and gambling rates are high. Fifty percent of construction workers are self-employed which can lead to job insecurity, especially as they get older[34]. Mental health issues are particularly relevant to elite sports people who are often under constant pressure to compete and succeed; injury is a major cause of stress and anxiety[35]. Elite sports people retire relatively young and are often left floundering about what to do with their lives. The chances of being a sports pundit on TV are few and far between. The partner we choose and the area where we decide to live, can all influence our mental health, not least indulging in illegal drugs such as cannabis.

---

32 Lifestyle Choices and mental health, BMC Pubic Health, 16 May 2018
33 Health and Safety Executive: Stress, Anxiety or Depression 2019
34 The Guardian 13 Aug 2019: Why do so many construction workers kill them-selves
35 Sports Medicine – Open: Mental Health and Elite Sport- A narrative, Souter, Lewis &Serrent

The Science Behind How Cannabis Affects the Functioning of the Brain.

The brain is made up of around 86 billion brain cells, known also as neurons. Each brain cell acts as a hub - receiving and passing on information. All of the 86 billion brain cells can instantly communicate with each other, sending millions of messages around the brain and the rest of the body. The reason cannabis can be so dangerous is that it can interfere with this process and distort the messages the brain cells are delivering to each other.

It is worth delving into this a little more to fully understand how cannabis interferes with the processing within the brain and why it can be so harmful. Our 86 billion brain cells are not physically connected to each other; there is a small gap between cells called the 'Synapse Gap'. This is where messages are transmitted from cell to cell. Each message is delivered across the synapse gap through 'neurotransmitters'. Neurotransmitters control which part of the brain the message should be sent to. So, for example, neurotransmitters can send a message to the muscles in your arm and fingers to pick out a sweet from a bag, then send a message to your fingers to place the sweet into your mouth, send another message to part of the brain - known as the 'reward' system, which enables you to savour the enjoyment of that sweet, and record that enjoyment for future reference.

Whilst your brain is doing all these things, neurotransmitters are also sending messages to the brain to enable you to process the plot of the film you are watching, and also remind you to switch your phone off - all at the same time! The brain has many types of neurotransmitters, each one processing multiple functions - controlling your heart rate, breathing, muscle movement, your moods, your thinking and many more. The one I particularly want to focus on is dopamine. Dopamine is the neurotransmitter associated with controlling our moods, thoughts and feelings - a clue to where cannabis comes in and why it can lead to schizophrenia, which is a mental illness affecting a person's ability to process thought!

As mentioned in Chapter 2, cannabis has a chemical called tetrahydrocannabinol, most commonly known as THC, which is the principal psychoactive constituent of cannabis and is what gives users the 'high'. One of the reasons cannabis is so potentially dangerous is that, when it is ingested either through inhaling or digesting, it goes straight into the bloodstream and within seconds is absorbed into the brain. THC has the ability to interfere with dopamine neurotransmitters and distort the signal, causing the neurotransmitter to send a surge of dopamine to the reward part of the brain which creates the immediate high.

This sounds good; however, the problem is that the effects of THC can stay in the brain, not just for hours, but days and even weeks. It is not just the high the brain has to contend with, but impaired memory, hand coordination, movement and behaviour. That is why it can be so dangerous to drive a car even days after taking cannabis. It is not only driving; if you work with machinery, your chance of an accident also increases. It affects your movement, concentration and your ability to process thought.

So it does not take a lot of working out that continued use of cannabis with high levels of THC can cause long term impairment to the communication systems of the brain. Indeed, scientists now know with reasonable certainty that long term use of cannabis, especially with high levels of THC, can lead to dependence, addiction and long-term damage to the brain. I will go into more detail on this later in the book.

Figure 2: A Single Brain Cell.

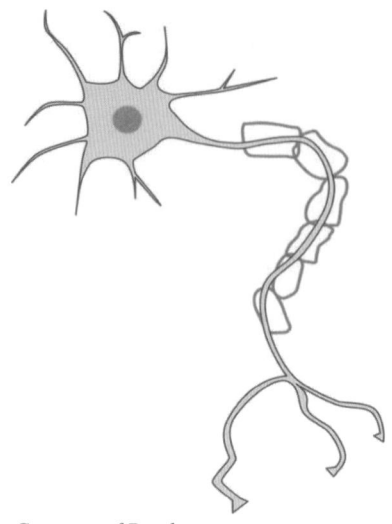

Courtesy of Pixabay

At the top of the brain cell is the point where the messages are received by the individual branches of the cell called dendrites, and the bottom is the long tail (the Axon) which transmit messages and where the dopamine is released, sending a message to the next cell.

Overleaf is a diagram of the synapse gap. At the end of the Axon is where messages are transmitted from one cell to another. You can see dopamine (the neurotransmitter responsible for moods and feeling) being released and received through the dopamine receptors in the adjoining brain cell. The THC in cannabis causes a flood of dopamine to occur, causing unnatural levels of euphoria.

Figure 3: The Synapse Gap

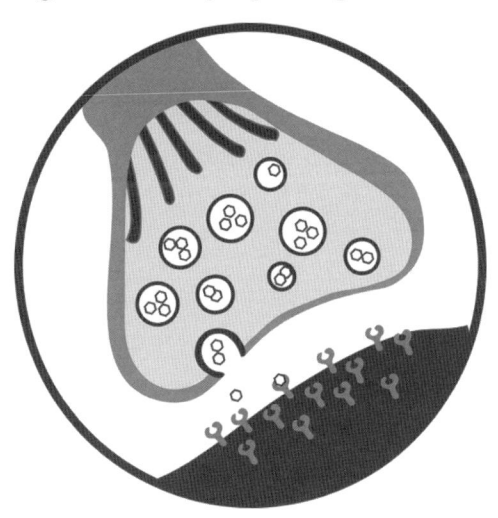

Courtesy of Pixabay

In the normal functioning of the brain, the flow of dopamine is carefully regulated so you are not constantly high – being uncontrollably high would be very inappropriate if you were at a funeral or at a job interview!

Understanding the causes of mental illness and how cannabis can interfere with the communication system of the brain is one thing - proving it is another matter. Thankfully that is precisely what scientists have achieved - they have provided us with the evidence.

Chapter: 4 The Hard Evidence We Have Been Waiting For

For years supporters of cannabis have rejected the many studies that link cannabis with psychosis, claiming that research has yet to fully prove a link. I was on a radio programme some years ago and was challenged to provide evidence that cannabis actually 'causes' psychosis. Well, of course I couldn't because 'causes' implies that the action of taking cannabis will definitely result in developing psychosis, in the same way that drinking arsenic will definitely end up in death.

It is impossible for any scientist to say that cannabis is a definite cause of psychosis because it depends on the individual's age, the dosage, gender, the genetic make-up.

There are simply too many variables to categorically state that if anyone uses cannabis they will, for certain, develop psychosis. What the scientists have been trying to do over the decades is to identify whether there is an 'association' or 'link' between taking cannabis and the development of psychosis, and that is precisely what they have now done. There is now a great deal more certainty that, if teenagers regularly use cannabis, they substantially increase the risk of damaging the development of their brains, which can lead to long term mental health issues, including schizophrenia.

That is why it is so disingenuous of supporters of cannabis to keep on repeating that cannabis does not cause psychosis or downplaying the dangers of cannabis. The tobacco industry used similar arguments in the 1950s, dismissing the studies which showed smoking was linked to cancer, and blaming pollution and people's lifestyles. Thankfully we now have the research on the link between cannabis and psychosis, which is now beginning to convince the sceptics.

Research Published in the US in 2017

After decades and hundreds of studies trying to identify a possible link between cannabis and mental illness, we now have the evidence. In 2017 the US National Academy of Medicine, a completely independent organisation and considered one of the foremost research organisations in America, issued a 468 page research paper entitled, **The Health Effects of Cannabis and Cannabinoids**[36].

They concluded:

Cannabis use is likely to increase the risk of developing schizophrenia and other psychoses; the higher the use and the younger the person is consuming cannabis, the greater the risk.

To produce the report, a committee of scientists and experts looked at more than 10,000 scientific abstracts and reached nearly 100 conclusions, covering the potential detrimental impact cannabis can have on people's mental and physical health. It also supported some therapeutic claims as well as throwing doubt on many others. The key findings of the study included:

On Mental illness the report states:

- *'There is substantial evidence of a statistical association between cannabis use and the development of schizophrenia or other psychoses, with the highest risk among the most frequent users. For individuals diagnosed with bipolar disorders, near daily cannabis use may be linked to greater symptoms of bipolar disorder than for non-users.*

---

36 https://www.nap.edu/catalog/24625/the-health-effects-of-cannabis-and-cannabinoids-the-current-state

- *Increased symptoms of mania and hypo-mania in individuals diagnosed with bipolar disorders.*
- *A small increased risk for the development of depressive disorders*
- *Greater frequency of cannabis use increases the likelihood of developing problem cannabis use.*
- *Initiating cannabis use at a younger age increases the likelihood of developing problem cannabis use'. (Children become addicted to cannabis.)'*

On Suicide:

'Heavy cannabis users are more likely to report thoughts of suicide than non-users'.

On Physical Health:

'There is substantial evidence of a statistical association between long-term cannabis smoking and worse respiratory symptoms and more frequent chronic bronchitis episodes'.

Driving Accidents:

'There is substantial evidence of a statistical association between cannabis use and increased risk of motor vehicle crashes'.

Children's Learning:

The report stated that there was a limited number of studies suggesting that there are impairments in cognitive domains of learning, memory and attention in individuals who have started smoking cannabis. The report also states that cannabis use during adolescence is related to impairments in subsequent academic achievement in education and employment.

The Benefits of Cannabis - Its Medical Use:

The report concluded that cannabis does have beneficial medical qualities including:

- *The treatment of chronic pain in adults. As antiemetics in the treatment of chemotherapy-induced nausea and vomiting (oral cannabinoids)*

- *For improving patient-reported multiple sclerosis spasticity symptoms (oral cannabinoids)*

- *There is moderate evidence that cannabis or cannabinoids are effective for: Improving short-term sleep outcomes in individuals with sleep disturbance associated with obstructive sleep apnoea syndrome, fibromyalgia, chronic pain, and multiple sclerosis (cannabinoids, primarily nabiximols).*

This was the evidence that many of us had been waiting for. It provided powerful evidence of the dangers of cannabis and more clarity about its benefits.

European Research Published in the UK 2019

More recently in 2019 another major study, **Cannabis Use and the Risk of Psychosis and Affective Disorders**[37] was undertaken by a team which included one of the world's foremost experts on cannabis and schizophrenia, Sir Robin Murray. This study produced compelling evidence of the link between cannabis

37 https://pubmed.ncbi.nlm.nih.gov/31647377/ (accessed: 24.06.20)

and serious mental illness, especially amongst teenagers. The study looked at 13 major studies that had taken place in different countries around the world. Ten of the studies confirmed the link while two showed a similar trend and one was not considered reliable. The study reported that the incidence of schizophrenia in South London had doubled between 1965 and 1999.

A very recent and large **Trans-European study**[38] has shown an eight-fold variation in the incidences of psychosis across 17 centres; the highest rates were found in London and Amsterdam, cities where young people have been reported to be taking the high potency cannabis. Indeed, in these two centres the use of high potency cannabis accounted for almost one-third and a half, respectively, of all new cases of psychosis.

The report went on to conclude:

> **Our findings confirm previous evidence of the harmful effect on mental health of daily use of cannabis, especially of high-potency types. Importantly, they indicate for the first time how cannabis use affects the incidence of psychotic disorder. Therefore, it is of public health importance to acknowledge alongside the potential medicinal properties of some cannabis constituents the potential adverse effects that are associated with daily cannabis use, especially of high-potency varieties.**

The message is now very clear; the stronger strains of cannabis which now populate Western towns and cities can damage the development of young people's brains, and refutes the arguments that cannabis is safe and does not cause severe mental illness.

---

[38] The Contribution of Cannabis use to variation in the incidence of psychotic disorder across EU-GEI: Marta Di Fort 2019

How Many People are Affected by Cannabis-Induced Psychosis?

Trying to establish the numbers of people treated for cannabis-induced psychosis in the UK is not straightforward. Many individuals are being treated in the community which means there are thousands of points where data has to be collected. Having so many points can result in data-collecting becoming more problematical. Even diagnosis can vary - one mother told me that her doctor said he would try and avoid giving her son a diagnosis of psychosis because it could affect his career prospects.

In 2018 the **Daily Mail** commissioned a report by NHS officials, and identified over a five-year period 125,000 people who were diagnosed with cannabis-induced psychosis[39]. I have spoken to experts who put a more conservative figure of between 7,500 and 10,000 cases per annum and, as mentioned several times in this book, it is young people who are particularly susceptible to cannabis-induced psychosis. I live in a rural area these days, having lived in and close to cities most of my life, so I am a little out of touch with 'city life', but a friend who still lives in London tells me that people are openly smoking cannabis in the streets, and he joked that you could get 'high' just walking down the road of some inner parts of London. People openly smoking cannabis is not just confined to big cities; only last month, I went for a walk through a park in Ashby-de-la-Zouch, a small market town in the Midlands, and saw a group of schoolchildren passing around a joint. I went to approach them, and they all jumped on their bikes and scuttled off.

This for me represents the heart of the problem we face and one of the reasons I wrote this book. Seeing young people unwittingly playing 'Russian roulette' with their mental health, with their future, with their parents' lives, pains me. I see flashes of Steve as

---

[39] Mail on Sunday, 13 October 2018. 125,000 people are admitted to Hospital over the Drug (cannabis) in just 5 years. Adams & Manning

a bubbling, vibrant young man, laughing and joking with his mates on the park bench, excited by life but with the dark shadow of cannabis-induced psychosis waiting to pounce.

Convincing the Public of the Hard Evidence

Trying to convince the public of the dangers of cannabis with hard evidence has been similar to trying to convince the public of the dangers of smoking tobacco seventy years ago - the evidence was clearly there but scientists and campaigners had to keep repeating the message. Smoking amongst men has dropped from around 70% for men and 40% for woman in the 1950s to, according to NHS statistics, 16.5% for men and 12.6% for women in 2019. Although cannabis use has dropped from the high of the 1990s, (see figure 1: Chapter 2) the use of cannabis amongst teenagers, especially the stronger strains of cannabis, now appears on the rise and it's the stronger strains of cannabis which can lead to serious damage to the brain. We cannot wait another 70 years for the message to slowly get across about the very real dangers of cannabis; every effort must be made to convince parents and their children. I will say more about this in Chapter 10.

Chapter 5 Cannabis: What Every Parent Needs to Know

I thought hard and long about the title of this book. I initially had doubts about including the word 'Parent' - was I being too forceful? Was I in danger of over-sensationalising? Was I exaggerating the dangers? (No!) The more research I undertook, the more I began to realise just how serious the situation is, and the very real danger increasing numbers of schoolchildren and young adults using high potency cannabis are in. The facts speak for themselves and therefore parents definitely DO need to know.

The Size of the Problem

In the UK cannabis is the most popular illegal substance across all age groups with a prevalence of five times more than any other drug used[40]. It is the illegal drug that teenagers first experiment with. In Suffolk children as young as 11 have been found using cannabis[41]. **Teenagers are more likely to have tried illicit drugs than smoking cigarettes – cannabis being the most popular choice**[42].

According to the 2018/19 NHS Digital survey of 193 UK schools, involving 13,664 pupils, a staggering 38% of 15-year-olds reported that they had tried drugs[43]. That means in a class of 30 children, 11 pupils will have used drugs, mostly cannabis. **One youth worker told me that some young people smoke cannabis like they are having a cup of tea.**

---

40 European Monitoring Centre for Drugs and Drug Addiction 2019 European drug report
41 East Anglia Times 30 may 2020
42 Damian Gayle Guardian, 2 Nov 2017,
43 NHS Digital, smoking, drinking and drug use among Young People in England 2018 (NS) 20 August 2019 National statistics, part 8&9

If we first look at the number of pupils in the graph below (fig 4) who admitted to ever having taken drugs, it increases with age, from 9% of 11-year-olds, to 38% of 15 year-olds, and this is not just boys; 22% of girls also admitted to trying drugs.

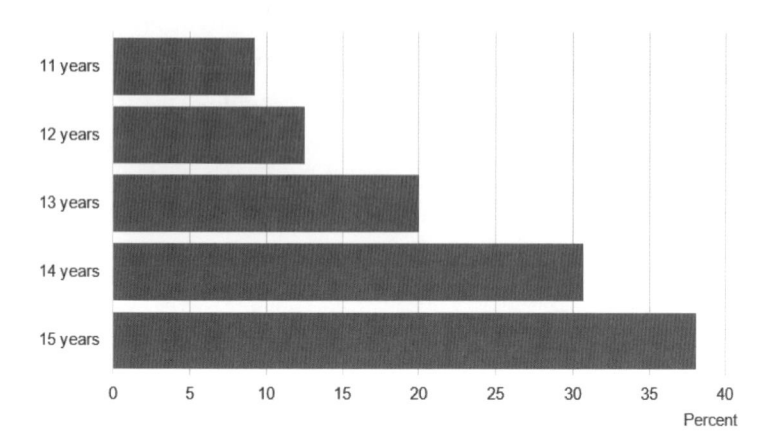

Fig 4: Pupils who have ever admitted to taking drugs

Age	Percent
11 years	~9
12 years	~12
13 years	~20
14 years	~30
15 years	~38

NHS Digital survey

The next graph, opposite (Fig 5), also taken from the NHS digital survey, shows cannabis is the most popular drug taken by schoolchildren in the last year. (Note: Volatile substances include solvents, glue and paint-thinners that young people inhale. Nitrous Oxide is laughing gas and is the latest craze; no doubt you will have noticed the little discarded silver canisters. New psychoactive substances are often known as legal highs which have been manufactured to mimic illegal drugs such as cannabis. They have only recently been added to the NHS survey, hence appearing as flat lines.)

Fig 5: Number of drugs and type of drug taken in the last year by schoolchildren

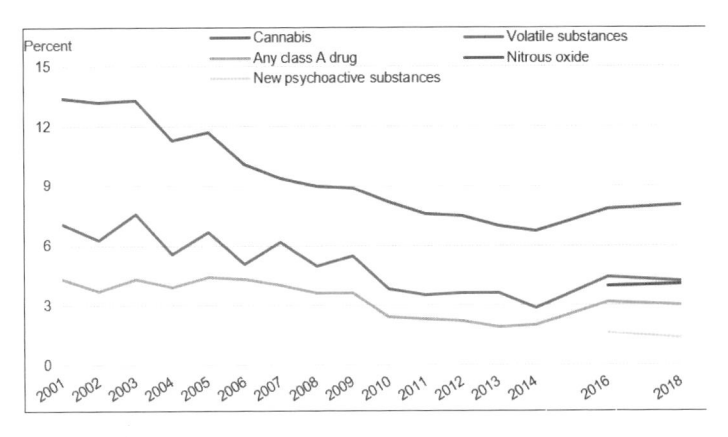

NHS Digital survey

The Fall and Rise of Cannabis

You will note that drug use amongst schoolchildren has dropped since 2000, which is in line with an overall drop in the use of cannabis, and which I reported in Chapter 2. This change in teenage behaviour could be down to a number of factors - more health awareness programmes taking place, schools being more proactive with drugs awareness, parents being more open about talking about drugs to their children, more media stories exposing the dangers and, of course, the increased number of research papers also exposing the dangers of cannabis. Governments can also take some credit. In 2003 the then Labour Government invested in a major cannabis/drugs awareness campaign called 'Talk to Frank'(www.talktofrank.com). The government substantially invested in major advertisement campaign with the media – TV, newspapers and cinemas. It also produced information packs for schools and advice to parents; it reached out to millions of young people. The website is still up and running. This campaign undoubtedly had a positive impact because, as you can see from the graph, cannabis use dropped dramatically at the same time that Talk to Frank was launched (2003). Unfortunately, cannabis use started to flat-line at the same time the Government decided to cut the Talk to Frank budget. Cannabis use has subsequently started to increase, so I will leave the reader to draw their own conclusions on the wisdom of cutting the Talk to Frank budget. (I will say a little more about this in Chapter 10.)

The Myth that Alcohol is Safer than Cannabis

If we now turn to the impact that taking cannabis is having on young people's health, we can begin to see why cannabis use is potentially a major Public Health issue. In a report by Public Health England: 'Young People's Substance Misuse Treatment Statistics 2018/19', 14,485 young people in the UK needed treatment for substance misuse; **88%** of these young people in treatment reported that cannabis was the main problem, followed by 44% who said it was alcohol. **Which contradicts those young people who say that cannabis is safer than alcohol; it most definitely is not!** A study in Canada of 3,826 young students (12 to 13) in 31 schools showed that cannabis use had a more lasting effect on a young person's brain than alcohol. It was found that cannabis use can lead to a decline in learning ability, decision-making and an overall decline in academic achievement which can last into adulthood[44]. The poor academic outcome has been linked to numerous studies linking cannabis use with a decline in the neurocognitive development of young teenagers' brains[45]. The outcome of this decline is that the brain does not develop to its full potential, hence the link

---

[44] A Population Based Analysis of the Relationship Between Substance Use and Adolescent Cognitive Development, American Journal of Psychiatry: on line 3 Oct 2018
[45] Adolescent Cannabis use, change in neurocognitive function and High School graduation, Ryan, Pingault Seguin, Dev Pyschopathoc, 2017 Oct 24

with poorer academic achievement. (I will say more about this in Chapter 9 when I talk about the hidden and subtle effects of cannabis.)

The science is now very clear: if a young teenager uses cannabis monthly, weekly or daily then they substantially increase the risk of damaging their brains; the more regularly they take it and the younger they are, the risk increases. By using cannabis, they are potentially gambling away their future lives. If cannabis caused premature baldness then I suspect young people would run a mile from it but, because the impact on their health is less obvious, kids blindly use cannabis, oblivious to the very real dangers that could be awaiting them. If they cannot see the dangers, then we adults have a duty to protect teenagers and young people from this dreadful modern scourge.

Cannabis and Black, Asian and Minority Ethnic Groups

Looking at cannabis use amongst 'Black, Asian and Minority Ethnic' (BAME) people, it does expose some worrying disparities and a few uncomfortable truths.

It is important to stress from the outset that people from BAME communities are not one homogeneous group. They are made up of a wide diverse number of people, including: Black Africans, Black Caribbean, people from India, Pakistan Philippines and Vietnam and many, many more.

The one thing that is common between BAME communities and with the rest of the UK population, cannabis is the most used illicit drug within these communities. But that is where the similarity ends.

It is when you look into the social inequalities and the way BAME people are treated by the criminal justice system do you realise that there are very serious disparities in the way white people are treated as opposed to people from BAME communities. When I studied this I was shocked to see just how minority groups have the odds stacked against them.

If you are from a BAME community, you are more likely to be stopped by the police - searched, prosecuted and sentenced for a drug offences than white people[46]. Black people are 9 times more likely to be stopped than a white person[47]. People from BAME communities are more likely to live in areas of greater social inequality.

Studies have shown that the 'criminal behaviour is linked to poverty, high unemployment and social deprivation[48]. As previously mentioned, recreational drugs, particular cannabis is used more in areas of high unemployment and social deprivation. According to the Social Metric Commission (reported by Patrick Butler in the Guardian, 1 July 2020) Nearly 50% of BAME households are living in poverty; let me say that again, because I had to read that startling statistic twice. Nearly 50% of BAME households are living in poverty. We seem to be inadvertently manufacturing crime by creating an environment for it to breed.

I was brought up in a single parent household with my two brothers, in a run-down part of south London during the 1950/60s. My mum was always in debt and struggled to pay bills. My brothers and I never thought twice to fiddle the gas and electric meters, to ensure we had heating and gas for the cooker. My eldest

---

46 UK Drugs Policy Commission: Drugs Diversity Ethnic Minorites Groups.
47 Victor Dodd, Police and Crime Correspondent Guardian, 27 Oct 2020
48 Haw, 1985:Peck and Plant, 1986 ab – GLA report: A Public Health Approach to serious Youth violence – Supporting evidence (15 July 2019 – Joseph Rowntree Foundation: Anti-Poverty Strategies for the UK (May 2014) .

brother had a part time job at a grocers shop; he often came home with packets of food hidden up his jumper. If we came across a stolen car that had been abandoned, we would be like vultures – taking off what we could to sell. Buying and selling stolen goods was the norm; it was away of getting things cheap or making a bit of money. The bottom-line is, my brothers and I indulged in delinquent behaviour, not because we liked breaking the law, but simply to improve our impoverished lives. Apart from a few close shaves, we never got caught – had we done so, our lives may well have turned out a lot different. Thankfully, we did not have covid, we did not have high unemployment and we had politicians, from all parties, that believed in the welfare state.

What chance then, has a young black kid got today; living in a rundown inner-city area, where unemployment is high and gang culture is rife. What chances do they have if they live in a dysfunctional household or worse being abused or brutalised. That need to survive, that need to improve their life is no different to the white kids in the 50s and 60s. But when the odds are stacked against you, when the gap between the rich and the poor is shamelessly obscene, is it any wonder young people in such situations turn to drugs to get some thrill out of life and to make money? I am not condoning it, simply explaining it. I have no doubt that many more of my generation would have turned to drugs and crime if faced with the level of social inequality, the level of unkindness and disregard many young people face to-day, especially people from BAME communities. John Lennon wrote, "All we need is love". I would also add, "All we need is empathy".

Perhaps now we can get a glimpse into why, in parts of London, 30% of all new cases of psychosis are linked to cannabis. Dr Shubulade Smith CBE, an award-winning British academic summed it up well in a report to the Schizophrenia Commission: *The Abandoned Illness (2012).*

> All those factors which combined to bring them (people with mental health problems) to my service may have been avoided. Is psychiatry the problem for most of my patients? Not where I work. It is imperative that we work at tackling the social inequalities that cause poor mental health. Doing so will undoubtedly improve the outcome for everyone, including those from BME groups.

> The evidence about social adversity and mental illness was striking. I look after people with severe mental health problems. I am frequently struck by how much they have in common. So many have experienced horrendous emotional trauma and significant social deprivation regardless of whether they were born in the Caribbean, Afghanistan, Surrey or around the corner in Lambeth. All too frequently I wish that someone had intervened when the person was 4 or 5- years old.

> All those factors which combined to bring them to my service may have been avoided. Is psychiatry the problem for most of my patients? Not where I work. It is imperative that we work at tackling the social inequalities that cause poor mental health. Doing so will undoubtedly improve the outcome for everyone, including those from BME groups.

This is a huge subject and I really cannot do it justice in this book. Suffice to say, there is an enormous amount of research out there highlighting the disparity between 'British White' and people from BAME communities. There is also plenty of good practise around the world which can demonstrate that most of these issues can be tackled and often reversed. It is essential, in my view, that all of us take serious notice of people like Dr Smith and the many who echo the same message. As I will show later on in the book, deprivation, cannabis and mental illness have also been linked to gang culture, violence and knife crime. None us can ignore these realities. Most of us want to leave the world a better place for our children. Having researched these issues I am absolutely convinced we could start to reverse the more sinister aspects of our society and begin to create kinder and more empathetic communities – time will tell.

Part 3

Chapter 6: Teaching Your Children to Avoid Cannabis

Introduction

Parents do not have the time to wait for governments to get their act together and produce large scale cannabis awareness campaigns. They must act now and get on with the job of teaching their children why and how to avoid cannabis and drugs generally. As parents we all understand the need to teach our children to look after themselves - not to get into cars with strangers, don't mix with trouble-making kids, stay away from rough areas, not get involved in gang culture; the list goes on. Teaching your children about cannabis is no different.

Understanding Why Your Child Would Want to Take Cannabis

There are many reasons your child would choose to use cannabis and it isn't just because it's fun and makes them feel good. One very important reason could be as a result of some underlying health issue; they could be depressed or suffering with a physical health problem. I heard about a family some years ago whose son started taking cannabis in his mid-teens. After months of heartache they discovered that their son had a cyst on his spine which was causing him pain. He took cannabis to relieve the pain and, once the cyst was treated, he stopped taking cannabis. I appreciate that this is a rare case but the point is, don't immediately assume your child's cannabis use is simply them being delinquent; look for other possible causes, including, bullying, low self-esteem, depression and problems at school. That's why it is important to talk to the school, college, workplace and also their friends first. Do a bit of detective work, especially if cannabis use seems very much out of character. There are many reasons why young people take cannabis, which include:

- It makes them feel good and it's fun
- Peer pressure
- Curiosity
- Natural rebellion and act of defiance
- Environmental, especially in areas of deprivation and high unemployment where drug use thrives
- Lack of confidence
- Misinformation - influencers telling them that it's safe, especially some people in the media

The following diagram explores which characteristics might be associated with having taken drugs in the last month. This identifies associations, not causes; in other words, factors which identify youngsters with an increased or decreased likelihood of having taken drugs in the last month.

Figure 6: Factors associated with taking drugs in the last year.

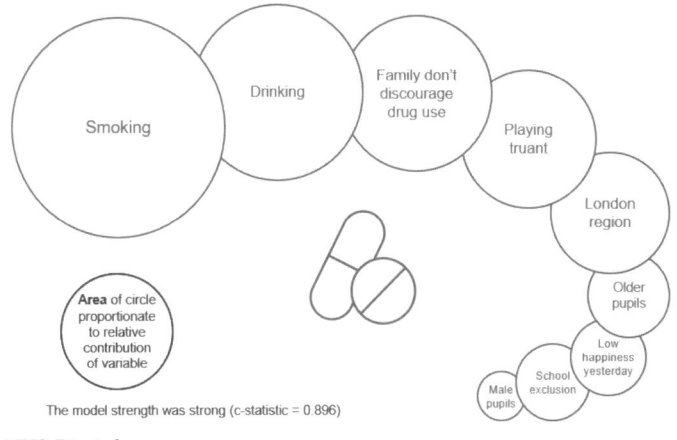

[Diagram showing circles of varying sizes representing factors: Smoking, Drinking, Family don't discourage drug use, Playing truant, London region, Older pupils, Low happiness yesterday, School exclusion, Male pupils. Area of circle proportionate to relative contribution of variable. The model strength was strong (c-statistic = 0.896)]

NHS Digital

When Do You Start Talking to Your Children about Drugs?

Educational experts suggest talking to children as early as possible; you can even start introducing them to the potential dangers involved from the age of three. This may sound completely daft but the suggestion is, not that you speak to them about illegal drugs-they obviously would not understand the concept - but about the need to make children aware of the dangers of putting in their mouths any tablets they might find. It is about having basic safety guidelines, explaining to them that the tablets are medicines taken for health reasons', they are not sweets and they must not touch them as it could make them very sick. I am sure most parents will have spoken to their children about this topic and, therefore, you will have already started talking to them about the dangers of drugs, albeit legal ones.

In respect of illegal drugs, and cannabis in particular, experts suggest the starting age can be between eight and twelve. This is the age they begin to understand the concept of what is 'socially' right and wrong, and will begin to understand what breaking the law means. It will of course depend on the child - some mature quicker than others. You know your child - it's your call - but please try not to leave it until they are teenagers when the hormones have kicked in, and when communicating with young teenagers can be more problematic. If you have not built up a rapport with your children by the time they are teenagers, then there is the danger that they are more likely to see you as out of touch, out of tune with their generation, not being "cool" and not knowing what you are talking about. That's why it is important to start communicating early so the question of drugs/cannabis becomes a natural subject to discuss later.

If the drugs subject has not previously been discussed and your children are already teenagers, it is even more important to raise the issue of cannabis and drugs. Don't sweep it under the carpet as one of those subjects best left unspoken because the issue could become a greater problem in later life when it might be much more difficult to deal with.

If there is already a problem of drugs and cannabis use in the family, it is even more important that the matter be raised. It will almost certainly require considerably more persuasion and energy to reverse a child's attitude to drug taking than it otherwise would have been if preventative action had been taken earlier. My family found this out the hard way, but the crucial message is that there are a multitude of actions that can be taken regardless of the situation a family might find themselves in.

Tips for Engaging with Children on Drugs Awareness

I hope the following comments will provide you with some useful tips to help you engage with your children to initially create a safe health and hygiene awareness, or to help prevent them from taking drugs or help restore their health following drug use.

Communicating with very young children (3-5 years)

During the pre-school years children have very strong ties to their parents and look to them for approval. It is a time when parents have considerable influence over their children because parents are much more central to a child's security and well-being. That is why it is an important time to start gently introducing the concept of basic hygiene and healthy life-style practice. By talking to them about health and well-being such as the need to clean their teeth, not eating the tablets in the medicine cabinet, awareness of talking to strangers, not eating too many sweets, managing their time on the computer, etc, it all becomes part of a child's on-going development. If you have already talked to your children about these issues, you will have started the process of introducing health education to your children and laying down the foundation that will enable you to talk about health and hygiene at a later age.

Dealing with Early Elementary Schoolchildren (5-8 years)

Children aged between 5 and 8 are still tied to the family but are beginning to explore their individuality, and are beginning to spend more time around other children and their friends' parents. They become more influenced by what is around them, what they see socially and through social media – television, films and video games. They are more likely to ask you leading questions; for example - why do you take the pills they see in the medicine cabinet? Why do you smoke? etc. If you are asked such questions, it is important that you respond as honestly as you can without, obviously, unduly alarming them. This will help to build up trust between you and your child. It is important that you don't ignore them or dismiss them for asking questions you don't think concerns them. That attitude will just lead to a child becoming less inclined to seek answers from you in the future, make them feel disengaged with you as their parent, and possibly encourage them to seek the answer from someone else whose views could be very different from yours, which may prove very harmful. Always try to find the time to answer your children's questions.

If, for example, you smoke and they ask you why you smoke, be honest and open with them. You can say that people don't always make the best choices as to what is good for them, particularly when they are young, subject to a lot of peer pressure and because smoking is very addictive - once started it can be difficult to break the habit. Each smoker will have their own story as to why they smoke but it is obviously important to get across the problem of addiction, and the link between smoking, poor health in general and perhaps cancer in particular. That's because it is recognised that smoking is addictive and bad for your health; the law recognises that young people need to be especially protected. For this reason, it is illegal to buy cigarettes under the age of 18 and the Police have the right to confiscate cigarettes from a young person under the age of 16.To repeat, the key thing is to engage with your children at an early age because it will enable you to talk more openly with them when they are older.

What to Say to Your Pre-teen About Drugs (9-12 years)

Children in this age group are beginning to find their own identity and will often value their friends opinions over that of their parents. It can be a frustrating and challenging time for parents. There is no simple formula for dealing with this age group because every child is different. However, there are some basic things you can do that may help:

1. When you decide to have a talk with your child, pick your time and make sure everyone has the time and is relaxed, not when your child is rushing off to go out. It's an important subject, so plan it.

2. Talk with other mums or dads about whether they have discussed drugs with their children; they may be able to give you some useful tips.

3. Ask your child whether they know about drugs and be prepared to give them answers, so do your homework.

4. Talk to your children about what they have watched, ask them what they think about it, especially if there was violence or a reference to drugs/cannabis. Help them to understand and differentiate between what is real and what is make-believe.

5. Always reassure them that you will be there if they need to talk about difficult subjects, such as drugs.

6. Avoid scare tactics; it is better to be honest and open with your children.

7. Make sure your child knows why there are rules and boundaries - that there are consequences if rules are broken and you'll enforce them. Research shows that young people are less likely to use tobacco, alcohol and other drugs if their parents have established a pattern of setting clear rules and consequences for breaking those rules.

8. Young people who don't know what to say when someone offers them drugs are more likely to give in to peer pressure. Let them know that they can always use you as an excuse and say: "No, my mum (or dad, aunt, etc.) will ground me for a month if I smoke a cigarette" or "My dad said that smoking will destroy my lungs and will affect my sport".

9. Get to know their friends and, if you have serious doubts about a particular friend, then you need to gently raise it with your child.

10. If you feel uncomfortable talking to your children about such difficult issues, then find someone, like a relative or friend, who might be able to help you. Grandparents are always a good fallback. You could always talk to the school or even your GP for advice. There are plenty of websites similar to the ones I have previously mentioned.

Talking about drugs to your children is one of the those 'big discussions' so you want to try and get it right. As I mentioned earlier, plan the discussion and do your homework – there is plenty of useful information contained in this book. It is probably unlikely at this age that they will have come into contact with anyone involved in drugs, but they would have almost certainly seen reference to them on the television, social media, etc. Remember, all you are doing is just 'flagging' up the issue at this stage, letting them know that you know about drugs, that they are very dangerous to children and that it is a subject ok to talk about.

Confronting the Issue of Drugs With Teenagers.

As teenagers develop, their mindset and attitudes become more and more influenced by influences outside their family. They will often be spending more time with school friends than with their parents, and will be living in a different world to their parents when it comes to teenage life, social media, music, video games, fashion and the like. It is a time when we parents are slowly shoved out of the centre of their lives, when they begin to feel they are centre of the universe, along with all their mates. To make things even more complicated it is a time when the hormones start to kick-in. So, approaching such a potentially toxic subject as cannabis needs to be done with considerable care. Having said this, and as I again repeat, the crucial message is that, if you follow some very basic steps, you should be able to communicate with your teenage child about cannabis, and you should be able to move the discussion forward.

Talking to Teenagers Who Have Not Tried Cannabis

If you have not already had the opportunity to talk to your teenage child about drugs in general and cannabis in particular, don't worry, it is definitely not too late. Biting the bullet, approaching the subject and discussing the physical and mental health, and social issues involved, can ultimately prevent a vulnerable teenager from potentially life-changing, highly negative experiences, in some cases wrecking their life. I hope the following will help guide you through some of the basic steps. I will be repeating messages I have given earlier and make no apology for this because the issue is so important.

1. As ever, plan the moment.
2. Pick your moment carefully and even rehearse what you are going to say, and think through what they might say back to you.
3. Try and remember what it was like when you were a teenager - show some understanding and empathy!
4. Stay calm and don't lecture, you will lose them if you do - as you have no doubt already experienced.
5. Explain why you are raising the issue of cannabis - the dangers.

6. Ask open questions to get things moving, such as "Do you know anyone who has taken cannabis at school?" Not, "Have you taken cannabis?" That is too direct. "Do your friends think cannabis is safe?" Note, the question is not asking them their views, but an opportunity for your child to come at it through their friends.
7. Tell them of your values about taking cannabis. That it can harm people especially young people, and that is one of the reasons why it is still illegal for young people in countries where cannabis has been legalised.

Remember the point of the exercise is to gently start a discussion on cannabis and for you to gauge their views on it and whether it could be a possible issue in the future.

The site www.drugfreekidscanada.org is an excellent website with considerable in-depth information about talking to teenagers and well worth exploring. When you read it, note that it is based in Canada. (See QR link below.)

Drug Free Kids Canada[49]

A second UK website, Family Lives, is also very good. It discusses the wider issues of talking to teenagers.

[49] https://www.drugfreekidscanada.org/wp-content/uploads/pdf/Cannabis-Talk-Kit_EN.pdf

Family Lives[50]

Dealing With Teenagers Who Are Already Experimenting With Cannabis - The Warning Signs - What to Look For and When

The average age teenagers start using cannabis is around sixteen, but we know teenagers will try cannabis as young as eleven. If you suspect that one of your children is using cannabis, then you can look for the following common signs.

- You may smell cannabis on their clothing
- Having red and bloodshot eyes
- Being a bit silly and acting out of character
- Having the munchies (picking at food)
- Appearing to be tired and lethargic
- Appearing to be anxious
- Look for signs in their bedroom such as roll-ups or small seeds of cannabis which are grass -like
- They are spending time with friends that you suspect could be cannabis users
- A sudden need for money
- A sudden use of mouthwash and air freshener in their room
- A drop in academic performance
- Not engaging in mealtimes

[50] https://www.familylives.org.uk/advice/teenagers/drugs-alcohol/talking-to-teens-about-drugs/

Steps You Can Take

It is important to stress that most teenagers will display some of these signs at some stage in their development, which does not mean they are cannabis users. But if you, as a parent, are concerned, then it is better to be safe than sorry. It may be a false alarm; that there is some other explanation for your teenage child's behaviour. If it is a false alarm, yes, your intervention could cause a row but, in my experience, it is far better to seek 'forgiveness than permission'. If you're wrong you can make it up to your child but, if you are right, your child is likely to be forever grateful for your intervention. Remember we parents are biologically programmed to protect our children; we are programmed to 'interfere', especially if we believe it will help them stay out of danger. Looking back on it, I wish I had the forethought to have intervened earlier with Steve; it may well have stopped him from wrecking his life and turning our lives upside down. But then, of course, we all wish we had the benefit of hindsight.

Many teenagers believe that cannabis is safer to use than alcohol, and that it is one of the more harmless drugs but it most definitely is not safer then alcohol for young people, especially very young teenagers. As I have pointed out, it can have a profound impact on young brains. It is important that when you talk to your children, you are able to give them the facts and come across as though you do know what you are talking about. But don't try and ram the facts down their throat. You can say to your child that, if they do not believe what you are saying, then Google 'Is cannabis safe to use?'. You could point them to the excellent government website 'Talk To Frank'[51] which is specially designed to relate to teenagers.

If you discover that your teenage child is using cannabis, the first

---

[51] www.talktofrank.com (accessed:25.06.20)

and most important thing to say is **don't delay** and put off having a discussion or taking action. If your teenage child has started playing around with cannabis, then your intervention could be one of the most important interventions your child receives in their lifetime. I am sorry if this comes across as alarmist, but parents cannot afford to take the risk of hoping that they will eventually grow out of it. As I have shown in this book, the cannabis on the streets today can be lethal for young people; it can be addictive and can cause long term cognitive damage to the brain. So, if your teenage child has started taking cannabis, then now is exactly the time to take action. Because the sooner you intervene the greater the chance of them stopping taking cannabis and reversing any potential dangers it could cause.

One mother I spoke to told me how she bitterly regretted tolerating their children smoking cannabis as teenagers:

> **"I thought at the time it was better letting them smoke cannabis at home instead of skulking off and smoking on a park bench. I genuinely did not realise how dangerous cannabis was at the time. I bitterly regret that now because both of them have developed mental health issues and one has sadly become a heroin addict."**

It is important you do not panic and rush in all guns blazing. Don't react as if they are full-blown addicts. Unless you have very good reason to believe they are using cannabis on a regular basis, or are showing worrying health signs (see next chapter), then assume they are just experimenting with it; experimenting is what teenagers do, they are wired up to experiment. If they admit they have tried it, then this is the time to 'nip it in the bud'. Remember, when you were a teenager and you had done something you knew your parents would be very angry about, you were probably feeling very anxious and worried. That is how your child is likely to be feeling. Being calm and showing some understanding will help to ensure you stay engaged with them and hopefully result in persuading them to stop.

In an excellent article by the psychologist Karen Young, ('Teens and drugs - What Parents Can Do. The signs. The Conversations. The response') [52], she talks about the importance of not being judgemental:

> "It is understandable that you might want to take a tough love approach, but the potential for this to drive your teen further into a drug culture is enormous. I have asked addicts the question, "What did your parents do that made it worse?" The typical response to this is something along the lines of, "they made me feel like I was a criminal". The more you criticise or judge your teen, the more they will move away from you and towards the people who really understand them – their drug buddies. Once that crowd gets a grip on your teen, they won't let go without a fight."

It is important to involve your spouse or partner; this is a very important issue you are dealing with, so you both need to be reading from the same page. Talk it through with each other before you talk to your teenage child. If you have a friend or someone in the family who you think could advise you, then use them, even if it means sharing your child's cannabis use outside the home. If it helps to stop your child using the stuff then so be it.

Don't assume that just one talk with your child will do the trick;

[52] https://www.heysigmund.com/teens-drugs-parents-need-know-conversation-response/

it may take a couple of conversations with them. Treat it as a marathon not a 100 metre dash. If you have a history of addiction in your family, or that of your partner, then be honest and open with your child; tell them that it could increase their risk of having an addictive personality which means that they could be more vulnerable than their mates.

One of the most important things to get across to your child is that you love them, and you do not want any harm to come to them; that is why you are pursuing it.

Many parents find it awkward to talk to their teenage children about such a 'difficult subject'. For some parents it will be the first time they have ever had to deal with such a major issue. It is therefore not surprising that it does not come easy. This is precisely why I wrote this book, because my wife and I did not talk about drugs to our kids; at best we felt awkward; at worst we were complacent.

The following are some suggestions for ways of approaching your teenage child, potential questions you could ask and responses they may give you. At the end of the day you are the expert on your child, you know them more than anyone else so you must decide what you think will work for you. The following are a few suggestions for tackling this delicate issue:

> 1. Think about when a good time would be to talk to them, when you know there is no pressure on time - possibly over dinner when your child is not engrossed in some activity - or on a car journey, or when they are in their bedroom. If you have a dog, then suggest taking the dog out together.

2. Once you have decided when, then start thinking about the how. You may decide that the best approach is to ask them direct. If you do, then it is important that you don't go in like a 'bull in a china shop' and cause sparks to fly all over the place. **It is essential that you do not let your emotions take control.**
3. The type of thing you could say is:
   "I need to talk to you about something which has been a worry to me. You are not in trouble; I just want you to be honest with me. I have smelt cannabis on your clothes, or I discovered signs of it in your room (or whatever it is that has raised your concerns)".
4. How do you respond if they say "it's none of your business and you should not be snooping around my room". You can say that it is very much your business because as a parent you have a responsibility to keep them away from harm. Remind them that you love them and that is exactly why you are raising it. You can also remind them that what they are doing is illegal and, if they are caught, they could end up with a criminal record which could affect their career chances, which you would not want to see happen.

Not telling the truth could be a real problem. The psychologist, Karen Young explains this well in the same article referenced above [43]:

> **"They have a good reason to lie and they will. Make it safe for them to tell the truth.**
>
> **It's likely that your teen will lie about what they are using, how much, or how long they've been using it.**

> **Initially, there will be more reasons for them to lie than there will be for them to tell the truth. They've found something that feels good and they don't want you to take it away – but you need to know what you're dealing with. For them to give up the information you need, they need to trust that you can deal with it. If your teen feels judged or criticised by you, there is no way they will open up to you and every chance they'll move deeper into the drug culture. Let them know that there is nothing they can say or do that will get them into trouble. This is about responding to the situation and guiding them, not punishing them for it."**

If they admit they have tried it, the first thing you want to say is "thank you for being honest". You could ask them why they tried it (see paragraph above 'Why your child would want to take cannabis'). You could then go on to talk about the dangers of cannabis. If you have examples of it affecting people you know, that will help to reinforce your argument, especially if it is a relative. You can talk about the impact genes have (see Chapter 3: The Role our Genes Play).

They might challenge you if you smoke, or they know you have tried cannabis or, indeed, are still using cannabis. Be honest and say people do stupid things and be prepared to say that you got it wrong! Tell them you don't want them to make the same mistake. Or you can say that, when they are an adult, they can then decide whether to use it or not, but it is definitely not safe, and you are not going to condone it.

What Happens if My Teenage Child Refuses to Cooperate?

If you teenage child refuses to talk to you, then remember - if they are under 18 you have parental control, it is your home, not theirs, so you make the rules.

If they are breaking the rules, then they must accept there will be consequences. One father told me that the most important thing they did was to ground their 15 year old son and stop his pocket money:

> **"We knew he was taking cannabis because we could smell it on his clothes. Eventually he admitted it and we were then able to start a sensible conversation with him. It took a few weeks of further conversation with our son, but he eventually got the message - stopped hanging around with the kids that used cannabis and stopped smoking it."**

Children and young people respond to clear direction and not to too many grey areas. It is important that you make it very clear from the start that you do not want them to use cannabis because it is unsafe, and that there will be consequences if they break the rules. One powerful sanction is to threaten to take away their phone and ban them from the computer. When my son-in-law threatened to take away my grandchildren's phones, when they both badly misbehaved, it was if he had cast a spell on them; they were immediately obedient!

Of course, it is not always that easy, especially if you are a single parent, but there are still things you can do, such as involve a friend, or close relative, an older sibling or perhaps someone you know who your child likes and trusts, such as a football coach, youth club worker or a particular teacher or lecturer at school/college.

You can move the conversation away from drug use if your child does not want to acknowledge there is a problem. You focus more on what changes you would like to see happen. Karen Young, again from her article referenced above said: (43)

> "If your teen doesn't want to acknowledge there is a problem, go with that and make it about the behaviours you're seeing, rather than the drug use. Acknowledge for now that there may not be an addiction or a problem, but that you would like to see certain behaviours increased (e.g. time with the family, other friends, activities, school work) and others decreased (drug use, time away from home, sleeping to recover from effects of use, violence, lying.)".

By shifting the discussion away from whether they are or not using drugs you are focusing on the behaviours which, if they are using drugs, will have altered, sometimes dramatically, over the time they have been using drugs. If they are under 18 then you have more power at your disposal to impose action to deter them particularly if they are very young teenagers.

There are also numerous organisations where you can get further information; some provide helplines:
- Drugfam: 03008883853, a national charity
- Support-line: 01708765200, a national charity
- Frank: 03001236600 which is a government-funded help line
- Adfam: 02038179410 (provides useful information and links to other resources)

If there are young people in the area that you know and who might have used it but have stopped, ask them to have a word with your child. Get someone you trust to help you to plan how you are going to approach it, and who could give you support.

If you already have a support worker or social worker, then ask them for help. Regardless of your situation, the continued use of cannabis by a young person will increase the risk of them developing health issues, especially mental health. Of course, not all people develop problems following cannabis use, but for those who do, it can go on to wreck their life and turn their own parents lives upside down.

As I have said previously, it will take time; having a one-off shouting match is unlikely to make much difference and possibly make things worse, so take your time and plan and prepare your response.

So, let's have a quick recap on approaching your child which you suspect is experimenting with cannabis:

1. Don't panic, try to be calm and measured.
2. Bring in help if you need it.
3. Do your homework, so you feel confident about talking about cannabis.
4. Plan what you are going to say and rehearse it.
5. Plan when and where you are going to talk to your teenage child.
6. Be prepared for the response your child might give.
7. Try and stay supportive and non-judgemental.
8. Make sure your child is clear that you are not prepared to condone using cannabis.

Obviously, your approach will be different depending on the age of your teenage child; dealing with a 13 year old is a lot different to a 19 year old. You have parental responsibility for the care and upbringing of your 13 year old; your 19 year old is an adult, and is responsible for his or her own actions. Having said this, if they are living in your house, they should be made to respect your rules. The same principles still apply about approaching your 19 year old and 13 year old. Be calm, do your homework, pick the right time, plan, etc.

One advantage of dealing with an older teenager is they will be a little more mature and street-wise. Discuss with them why they take cannabis, tell them you are genuinely interested in understanding why they are using it. If you start to judge them and come down heavy on them, you are in danger of shutting down the conversation and that's the last thing you want to do. If you manage to have a conversation which is not a shouting match and reasonably calm, you could ask them:

- What is it they get from taking cannabis?
- Do they feel that it is helping them to get to where they want to be?
- Do they feel that taking cannabis has changed them in any way?
- What are the upsides?
- What are the downsides?
- You could point out how you see things have changed

If you have managed to get to this point without the conversation falling apart, then this is a very positive sign. You may say to them that, if they are feeling under pressure or uncomfortable, then you are happy to stop the conversation and maybe pick another time.

As I said, this process of turning things around is a marathon, not a 100 metre dash.

If there are obvious signs of cannabis use, such as change in behaviour, their appearance and their health, then tell them. They may be completely oblivious to any changes. It may be a wake-up call, especially if others have noticed and have told them.

When my son was using cannabis, which at the time we were unaware of, I noticed he was staying in his room a lot more. He became much more secretive, he started missing college, and refused to engage with my wife and me. At the time, I thought he was getting depressed because of pressure from college and his girlfriend packing him up, but we now know that was the start of cannabis affecting his mental health. By the time we fully intervened it was too late, he had started to develop psychosis.

If you are at the point where you are concerned that your child or a close relative is using cannabis and you want more in-depth information on what to do, then I encourage you to read the article by Karen Young, previously mentioned. I attach a QR link to it. I thoroughly recommend you reading it as it will reinforce a lot of the things I have said in this book and what the various charities I have mentioned say. Also, the organisations I mentioned earlier with the QR links (Drug Free Canada (41) and Family Live (42) also provide useful information.

Karen Young: What Parents Can Do - The Signs. The Conversation. The Response.

Summary

Having looked for the signs and believing your teenager may be taking cannabis, it is important that you act as soon as you can and not put it off. It is essential to stay calm and not to lose you temper. Plan where, when and how you are going to approach them. Decide on the type of questions you might ask them and be prepared for the possible responses they might give. Make sure you set the rules and boundaries, so they know exactly where they stand but, at the same time, tell them that it is because you love them, and do not want harm to come to them. Lastly, if you feel daunted by the task then get help from someone close to you, or seek professional support from one of the organisations I have mentioned.

Part 4

Chapter 7: What to Do when Cannabis Takes Hold

The Warning Signs
When cannabis use triggers mental illness and in particular psychosis, the symptoms often set in quickly and without much warning. The following are some of the key signs to look out for:
- An unusual drop in their commitment at school, college or work and in their daily activities
- Shutting themselves in their room
- A change in sleep or appetite
- Difficulty with memory, thinking and other mental tasks
- Having exaggerated beliefs about personal powers or magical thinking
- Feeling disconnected from surroundings
- Heightened sensitivity to sight, touch, sound or taste
- Loss of desire, and being apathetic
- Mood changes (depressed and anxious)
- Paranoia and fear of others
- Their behaviour has been unusual
- Withdrawal or loss of interest in activities
- Muttering to themselves
- Dropping out of college or losing their job

The Steps You Can Take
Again, I must emphasise that, even if your child is showing some of the above warning signs, it doesn't necessarily mean that they are suffering with psychosis or the side effects of cannabis; they may simply be suffering with the effects of being a 'teenager', particularly if they are shutting themselves in their room, dropping out of college or having problems with work. Your child might

just be getting a little depressed over something. They may not want to talk to you about it but, all the same, you need to keep an eye on them and perhaps talk to people who know your child, and ask them if they think they are OK. I would certainly talk to the school or college who have a duty of care to share information with parents if it is in the 'interest of the child's health'. If they say they cannot discuss such information because of confidentiality, remind them that you will hold them personally responsible if your child's health deteriorates and they do not share this with you. In most cases schools and colleges are pretty switched on to their 'duty of care', but some are less so.

In many cases young people who smoke cannabis can experience short-term side effects and will recover. However, it is better to be safe than sorry, even if the side effects disappear. The very fact that they experienced them in the first place could be a warning sign that their brains are not coping with cannabis well. If the symptoms continue or return and there is a continued change in their mood and behaviour, I would start to get worried, especially if these changes continue for two to three weeks or more. If they are showing signs of anxiety, paranoia, muttering to themselves - the more explicit signs of severe mental illness - then don't wait, seek immediately help as you need to get your child assessed.

Making the First Step to Getting an Assessment

I appreciate it's a cliché to say, 'making the first step is going to be the hardest step' but, if you are in the situation where you are really concerned about your child's mental health, then making that first step can be truly the hardest step to make. It can be the most frightening situation any parent finds themselves in. I felt physically sick when I first realised I was going to have to seek help for my son; for some people it may be all too much to bear or could lead to a state of denial.

The hard facts are that, if your child is showing symptoms of serious mental illness, then it is essential that you get them properly assessed, and the quicker you do that the better. As mentioned previously, early intervention is absolutely essential. Your first step should be to talk to your GP, because they are the route into the mental health services, and it is where your child can receive a proper assessment. Remember, it's the assessment you are after, and that is what you want your GP to help you with.

I understand that some people may find it all too difficult to talk to the GP. If you find that you can't bring yourself to contact your local surgery, then talk to one of the mental health helplines, such as Rethink Mental Illness (0300 500 0927), or the SANE help line (0300 304 7000) and Mind (0208 519 2122). They will be able to talk to you over the phone, in confidence and guide you through what you need to do. Sometimes talking to an experienced listener can help you feel more relaxed and more confident. The bottom line is, if your child is experiencing mental health problems, then **it is essential that you seek help immediately. In the same way, if your child was showing a high fever, you simply cannot afford to delay.**

Contacting Your GP
Sometimes it can take weeks to get an appointment. However, if you struggle to get one, tell the receptionist that your child or adult is showing the signs of serious mental health problems, and you believe their mental health is seriously at 'risk of deteriorating'. You could even say, if you are still struggling to get an appointment, that you are worried about self-harm (this can

happen, and does happen, to people experiencing the early signs of mental illness; my son started bashing his head against a wall to try and get rid of his voices). Don't allow the receptionist to put you off and delay the appointment. If you are worried that you might find it difficult to be assertive, then get some other member of the family to ring the surgery - with you standing by their side.

The message you want to get across is that you believe your child's mental health is **seriously at risk**. Make sure you can back that up with examples of their behaviour. If you are convinced your child is smoking cannabis, tell them. Likewise, if your child is displaying signs of psychosis, tell them that you believe, for example, they are becoming paranoid, possibly hearing voices, becoming depressed or whatever you believe the case to be. It is essential that you get across the sense of urgency and, as previously mentioned, don't be talked into putting it off. It is also important that you stay as calm as you can. The receptionist is only doing their job. Your job is to convince the receptionist that this is a very real emergency. They may suggest a telephone appointment - although face to face is better; if it means talking to a GP that day, then accept it.

If you have a good rapport with your child, talk to them before making the appointment. Ask them about the way they are feeling, if anything is worrying them, have they got thoughts in their head that they don't like? Are they feeling anxious? Ask them if they would like you to try and help with any unwelcome thoughts or feelings. You could ask them what do they think could be causing their concerns, and that you have heard that some people have a bad reaction taking cannabis - do they think it could be that? Obviously, you have to be very careful when talking about such things; you know your child so you will be the best judge. The general rule is to stay calm, be very supportive and, whatever you do, don't be judgemental and critical; remember your child may well be in a very frightened state of mind. Your child will need a lot of support and above all, love. If your child is able to tell you their concerns, then this is crucial information you can use when you talk to the GP.

When my son first become psychotic, he refused to engage with us, just saying, "I'm all right, it's nothing". We ignored this because we knew something was wrong and eventually got the doctor to visit him. I was convinced that Steve was secretly relieved that the doctor spoke to him because he knew deep down things were not right.

Once You Get an Appointment With Your GP
Once you get the appointment to see your GP, write down all the things that are concerning you and why you think your child is beginning to suffer with severe mental illness. Better still, keep a diary and record the incidents of odd behaviour - I did this prior to talking with the GP. It worked! I read to the doctor a few incidents which were concerning us and he immediately got the message that things were not right.

The following list may help you structure your visit:
- Explain your child's symptoms and behaviour
- Time-frames: when they first started, and if/when they escalated
- Any triggers you can identify
- The impact the difficulties are having on your teenage child, the rest of the family, their school life, college or work place, etc
- Be clear what outcome you are hoping for; be very specific, for example: "I would like my child to undergo a mental health assessment".

What Happens if You Are Told that Your Child Cannot be Treated Until They Stop Taking Cannabis?

Well, they are wrong! When someone has a mental health problem and is using drugs such as cannabis, then they are classified as having a 'Dual Diagnosis', i.e. a serious mental health problem and a substance problem. According to the National Institute for Clinical Excellence, the local Health Service **must** take responsibility for both conditions and will arrange for the appropriate intervention. If you do experience problems then, again, contact one of the helplines previously mentioned. Rethink Mental Illness has a very good fact sheet on Dual diagnosis.[53]

If your doctor agrees with you that your child does need an assessment and your child is under 18, they will be referred to 'CAMHS' (Child and Adolescent Mental Health Services'- see below). If they are over 18, then the assessment will be done through your local 'Adult Mental Health Services' which is a specialist service dealing with mental health issues. Your GP will organise this for you. I will cover more about CAHMS later.

It is worth mentioning that if your child's health deteriorates and you become concerned that they are in immediate danger - particulary of self-harm or even suicide - then don't wait until this becomes an emergency.

According to the NHS's own website these conditions should be treated as an emergency in the same way as a physical health emergency - so either ring 999 or take your child to your local A&E. I appreciate that some people may feel reluctant to do this but, if your child's health is seriously deteriorating and you are genuinely worried that things are getting out of control, then you

[53] https://www.rethink.org/factsheet-download/?f=https://www.rethink.org/Factsheets/7060/Drugs,%20alcohol%20and%20mental%20health%20factsheet (accessed: 26.06.20)

have no choice but to take immediate action by contacting the emergency services.

What Happens When Your Child is Over 18 and Refuses to Cooperate?

If your child is over 18 and refuses to cooperate or, even worse, insists that you do not contact the doctor, then I am afraid you will have to override their demands if you genuinely believe that they are showing signs of serious mental health problems, particularly psychosis. It's either respecting their demands and possibly allowing their condition to get worse, or getting them treatment. I have always taken the view that it's a case of 'tough love'. If you believe your child is in real danger then you have no choice but to take action. If your adult child refuses to cooperate and will not see any one and you consider their health is badly deteriorating, then you may have no choice but to use the 1987 Mental Health Act, which was revised in 2007. Section two states:

> **'If the person is potentially suffering from a mental disorder of a nature or degree which warrants their detention in hospital and that it is in the interests of the person's own health, their safety or for the protection of the people** [54].'

Note the phrase, **'It's in the interest of the person's own health'**. So even if they do not pose a danger to themselves or others, if it's in the interest of the individual's health, then health professionals have a legal duty to take this into account. I appreciate that Chapter 2 refers to being sectioned and admitted to hospital; the point being, until your adult child is properly assessed, will the medical team know how to deal with them? My son, who was over 18 at

---

54 https://www.lscft.nhs.uk/section-2 (ACCESSED: 25.06.20)

the time, refused to cooperate. The very threat of being sectioned was enough for him to meet up and talk with the GP. I felt dreadful doing this to my son but, looking back on it, it was definitely the right thing to do. If you get to that point and your adult child still refuses to cooperate, then use the full force of the Mental Act if it is the only way. This is where charities such as Rethink and SANE can be very helpful in advising and supporting you.

Dealing with Children Under 18

For children under 18, the NHS has a specialist unit called 'CAMHS' (Child and Adolescent Mental Health Services'). CAMHS provides help for young people with a range of difficulties, including mental health problems and emotional problems. CAMHS are able to offer assessments, diagnosis, treatment and support for children, and young people. They are also able to provide support and advice to parents. The most common way to get a referral to CAMHS is through your GP. Your GP has to see your child in person, so you could either book a double appointment and see the GP first by yourself, and then bring your child in from the waiting room, or book a single appointment on your own first, and then take your child at a later date.' Children can also be referred to CAHMS by the school, college or health visitor.

Getting an appointment may take time as they prioritise the cases which are most urgent. It can take several weeks to get an appointment with CAMHS, sometimes months. You must try and ensure, with the help of your doctor, school or social worker, that you have identified all your concerns about your child to CAMHS. If you are concerned that the delay is seriously putting them at risk, such as suicide or self-harming, then make sure CAMHS are aware of this – it is always best to put such concerns in writing and copying in the GP. Likewise, if you are concerned about your safety or the safety of others, make sure all parties are aware. Don't hold back, the more CAMHS are aware of the level of urgency then the greater likelihood of getting a more urgent appointment. You may be told that there are lots of urgent cases, and your child is just one of those cases. That is not your concern; your concern is your child and their safety.

One mother said to me when she was waiting for help from the Mental health services:

> "I needed rescuing; I was adrift in a storm, waves were crashing down on me. I was holding onto my son for dear life while watching him drown in his psychosis. I was exhausted, crying out for help and no-one was coming."

The mother was rescued, but only after the mother put her son in the car, and took him to the local hospital, and refused to budge until someone saw them. Hopefully, you will not have to take such desperate action.

Once you have got an appointment with CAMHS, they will ask you to bring your child for an assessment. That's fine if you can get your child to leave the house, so don't be surprised if they refuse - CAMHS will be used to this, so you may need CAMHS to do a home visit. If you tell them that your child refuses to come out of their room, or is frightened to be with strangers, then they should understand the dilemma you are in.

It may well be that a talk from a health professional to your child about using cannabis might be enough for your child to stop using it. If they do stop, the bad effects of cannabis might wear off and your child's mental health stabilises. If your child is in the early stages of smoking cannabis, then there is a higher chance of a quicker recovery. However, if your child has been using high-potency cannabis for some time, than the damage to your child's mental health could take longer to stabilise. As I have previously mentioned, early intervention is paramount as it is with most physical conditions; if you notice a lump in your breast or on the side of your neck, you don't ignore it, you seek immediate help - mental health is no different.

Preparing for the CAMHS Assessment

In the same way as you would prepare to visit the GP, you should also prepare for the assessment. Some children are very good at covering up their symptoms and will produce an Oscar-winning performance at the assessment, trying to demonstrate how normal they are. Experienced assessors should see through this. However, if you produce your own evidence, then it will make the assessor's job that much easier.

The evidence you could provide:
- Extracts from your own observations, including your diary if you have kept one
- Evidence from what their friends have said
- Evidence from the school or college. (I recently spoke to a head teacher and asked her whether she would be prepared to share private information about a child to a parent. "Of course I would; I have a 'duty of care' to do so if the child is under 18".)
- Conversation you may have had with your son/daughter about his/her thoughts, feelings and behaviour

I would send the evidence before the assessment. You may want to ask CAMHS not to say to your child that you have sent it, the reason being that if your child is suffering with paranoia and becomes aware you have been 'talking about them', it may reinforce any paranoia thoughts they may have about you and other members of the family.

Don't be frightened to ring up CAMHS and ask them to talk through the process with you. This is going to be a completely new experience for you and your family so it is important to get yourself prepared. Speak to a local carer's or family group to see if anyone there has experience of dealing with CAMHS. Young Minds (part of the National mental health charity MIND) have a very good fact sheet on CAMHS - see the QR link below:

Young Minds CAHMS guidance[55]

What happens after the Assessment?

Once your child has had an assessment either through CAMHS or the Adult Mental Health Services, if your child is over 18 a decision will be made about whether they require some form of intervention. If they do, then they will be assigned a 'Treatment Plan'. The plan will take into account the needs of your son or daughter which will depend on the severity of their illness. As a general rule, if your child is displaying acute signs of psychosis - delusions, hearing voices, paranoia, acute anxiety - then they may decide to prescribe medication in the form of anti-psychotic drugs. These will help to manage the symptoms. Certainly, when my son was prescribed antipsychotics, they made a remarkable difference - we got him back from a complete state of madness - it was as if tentacles that had been gripping his mind; crushing-reality; had been made to relax its grip - the psychosis did not go but was less acute.

If your child is not displaying acute signs of psychosis, the health professionals may prescribe a course of psychotherapy. Psychotherapy or talking therapy focuses on helping the individual control their emotions and behaviour, their exaggerated thoughts and anxiety. Psychotherapy is not normally used to treat psychosis on its own although more recently, a form of psychotherapy called CBT (Cognitive Behavioural Therapy) has been developed, specifically to work alongside antipsychotic drugs. The benefit of this is, if it works for the individual, it may be possible to reduce the level of medication, bearing in mind that antipsychotic drugs are not without their side effects.

It is important to stress that treating mental illness is not an exact science. It is a highly complex condition and can vary according to individual make up, so certain interventions may work for some young people but not for others. Often, getting the right medication and dosage can be a matter of trial and error, so be patient and accept that it may take time to get the right intervention in place.

Receiving a Diagnosis

Very often young people who have been assessed following regular use of cannabis are diagnosed with 'cannabis-induced psychosis'. Someone given a diagnosis of psychosis may recover once they have stopped smoking cannabis or are given a course of psychotherapy; talking therapy is one of the interventions. But if they don't respond and the psychotic symptoms continue or get worse, especially if they continue to use cannabis then, like my son, they may be given the diagnosis of schizophrenia, (schizophrenia and psychosis are related - both conditions overlap). The main difference is that a person can become psychotic if they have bipolar or some other mental health condition, whereas schizophrenia is a specific condition where psychosis is one of the symptoms.

Whilst schizophrenia can sound like a very scary and frightening diagnosis, it is treatable and, although there is no specific cure, many people with schizophrenia do stabilise over time and go on to live productive lives, as my son has done. According to the mental health charity SANE, only 8% of people with schizophrenia are in full-time employment. However, according to the National Institute of Mental Health in the US, around fifty percent of people with schizophrenia can function independently; it is only a small percentage of people with schizophrenia who require ongoing care and support.

If your child is given a diagnosis of schizophrenia, there is considerable material out there to inform and educate you about the condition, but I would urge you to look at the more reliable websites such as the NHS, Rethink Mental Illness, Mind and SANE. I have also mentioned Fuller Torrey's book: **Surviving Schizophrenia - A Family Manual**; again, another important resource and one I wish I had read earlier.

It is also important that you get other members of your immediate family to read up on the condition because then the burden can be shared. This will help with your mental well-being and hopefully reduce the overall fear and foreboding - knowledge and understanding are vital tools in the battle to gain stability and hope. If you do not have an immediate family or a family that does not want to engage, as mentioned, seek out support through a professional health care worker or, if possible, through a carer's group or perhaps another family in a similar situation. Health care workers might be able to connect you with this support. Also, make use of one of the various mental health charities with helplines mentioned above, because your situation is precisely why many of them were set up in the first place.

Chapter 8: Treating Psychosis

The Treatment Options

Once the doctors have given a diagnosis, they will then look at the treatment options. It will of course depend on many factors, not least the severity of the illness. Normally, schizophrenia and/or psychosis is treated with antipsychotic drugs. If the condition is less severe, then they may use psychotherapy. The main difference between antipsychotics and psychotherapy is that antipsychotic drugs interact with the brain's chemistry to alter the activity of the neurotransmitters (Chapter 3). The psychosis is thought to be connected with the level of dopamine in the brain; antipsychotics alter the flow of dopamine, helping to relieve the unpleasant symptoms of the illness.

Psychotherapy helps the individual to become more aware of the upsetting thoughts, and to learn how to manage those thoughts. Very often antipsychotics and psychotherapy are used together, the former to stabilise the brain chemistry and the latter to help the person have insight into their condition, and the impact cannabis is having on their mental health.

It is worth mentioning that there are different types of antipsychotics and, if your child is put on them, then you need to be aware that they can have different side effects. Antipsychotics can be divided into 'first generation' drugs which were developed in the 1950s, and 'second generations' drugs which were developed later. The main difference between first and second generation drugs is found in their side effects. Second generation antipsychotics have, in the main, less unpleasant side effects than the older first generation drugs. The reason first generation drugs are still used is because in some cases the older drugs, for some patients, can be more effective than the new drugs but, in the main, second generation antipsychotics are preferred by patients because of the side effects. The side effects of first generation drugs include restlessness, drowsiness, 'the shakes' and movement of the jaw, mouth and tongue. One of the less welcome side effects of the latter, second generation drugs, is that some can cause weight gain and fatigue.

The job of the psychiatrist is to try and find the optimum balance between treating the illness and minimising the side effects. Your job as a parent, and that of your child, is to help the psychiatrist reach that balance by giving them feedback. It can take time to get the right medication and the right balance; one particular medication may work for one person but not another, so it can be a case of trial and error. This can cause a lot of frustration for parents and indeed the patient, but unfortunately that is the nature of the condition. It is a matter of being patient and sticking with it.

First generation drugs include:
- Haldol
- Loxitane
- Mellaril
- Moban
- Navane
- Prolixin
- Serentil
- Stelazine

Second generation drugs include:
- aripiprazole
- clozapine
- olanzapine

- quetiapine
- risperidone
- ziprasidone

Non-Compliance

Non-compliance can be a problem, especially early on (patients refusing to take their medication). Some patients may even believe they don't need medication. This is not uncommon, especially for people who don't have insight into their illness. In their confused state of mind, they may believe that they are not ill and that it's all a conspiracy caused by 'dark forces'. This can pose a challenge to the doctor and to parents. At the time it may seem absolutely logical to a patient; if the patient does not believe they are unwell, then they will reasonably ask themselves, "Why should I take medication if I am not unwell?" A real 'Catch 22' situation. It is important to stress these challenges are all very well known to health professionals and there is an array of interventions that can be used to overcome them. So, if you find yourself in that situation, ask the GP what intervention they are going to use and whether you and the rest of the family can help.

Self-Medication

Self-medication is another one of the challenges doctors are often confronted with. I mentioned earlier, where someone may be taking cannabis to mask an underlying health problem, they may be depressed or anxious about something and find that cannabis temporarily relieves those unpleasant feelings. But all too often the underlying problem returns once the cannabis has worn off and the individual again turns to cannabis, and so the cycle goes on with the individual unwittingly making things worse and worse. They can become so deluded that they genuinely believe that cannabis is the only thing that alleviates their unwelcome thoughts and feelings, blind to the fact that cannabis is making things worse. Cannabis, or to be more specific, the THC, is seriously damaging the brain's 'wiring' system.

It is the same with drugs generally - heroin, crack, ecstasy and even excessive alcohol - the more you take the more your body needs it. Continuous overuse can lead to addiction and eventually a spiralling down into an abyss - which can also happen to some cannabis users. If you find your adult child is struggling to accept medication or is adamantly refusing to take it because they do not accept they are ill, then this is where the health professionals can intervene. Initially they may be able to persuade your adult child to take medication but, if they are adamant and at risk of continuing to be locked into a psychotic state, then the health professionals will need to take more direct action, such as hospitalisation. As I have already noted there are interventions that can be used to help the individual gain insight through the use of psychotherapy. It may take time but psychotherapeutic interventions can (and do) work very effectively.

My son still smoked cannabis on and off for the first year during his treatment, but the intervention from the medical team gradually helped him to relate his unpleasant thoughts and feelings with the use of cannabis. I distinctly remember him saying to me one day, "Dad, I am certain that cannabis is mucking my head up." So, with a combination of professional intervention and his own instinct for self-survival, he stopped taking cannabis.

It was the psychiatrist who eventually persuaded my son to try medication to reduce his bad thoughts and feelings. After three or four attempts with different antipsychotics, Steve finally settled with one whose symptoms he was prepared to tolerate - Olanzapine. Within two or three weeks of taking this medication, we noticed a difference. He became less psychotic and manic, which meant our life became less fraught. All this did take time - it took longer and was more problematic than we had anticipated - but by hanging on we finally got there. Much of this was due to the brilliance of Steve's psychiatrist, Professor David Kingdon. We will always be in his debt for rescuing Steve from the abyss and showing such kindness and understanding to the whole family. One of the most important things Professor Kingdon did was to listen to us. He made us feel that we were part of the team and, when things were going badly, he or a member of his team would always respond and guide us through that particular mini-crisis. He found the right medication for Steve and arranged the talking therapy which proved such an important milestone. I am convinced that involving us made all the difference to our well-being and Steve's.

Communicating with Your Child who is Refusing Medication.

If you are in the situation where your child or adult teenager is refusing to take medication, particularly if they believe they are not unwell, and are convinced external forces are causing their nasty and unwelcome thoughts, then try not to contradict them. At the time I was advised to not go along with his psychotic beliefs. It was suggested that I support my son by saying something like "I understand why you don't think you are unwell and that dark forces are at work, but that is not how I see it". I said to my son that I believed that was how he was feeling, but I gently tried to persuade him to question the logic of what he was saying; "why do you think the dark forces are only talking to you and not me or your sister?" Having said this, I did not push it too much, mainly because I felt

I was getting a bit out of my depth and I knew, if I pushed it, it would make him angry.

Remember, schizophrenia is a very powerful condition which fools the mind into believing the delusions are real. When people with schizophrenia say they are hearing voices, they truly are hearing voices, albeit generated from the mind. It appears that the brain's wiring system is malfunctioning and somehow misinterprets internal thoughts with the external sound, such as speech. So, the individual is fooled into believing their thoughts are actually external speech. The science behind this is complex and not fully understood but, whatever the science is, accept that people do hear voices, and their voices can cause a lot of distress. Medication can reduce that distress and help people to manage their voices. That is why it is crucial to persist with trying to get the right medication/ intervention so they do not linger in a psychotic state for too long.

Getting a Second Opinion

If you, your child or your adult teenage child is unhappy with the diagnosis or indeed with the medication which has been prescribed, then you can ask the GP or Psychiatrist for a second opinion. They **'do not'** have a legal duty to provide you with one, but they do have a responsibility to listen to your concerns and explain why they are taking the approach they have. In most cases doctors are more than happy to do this. If you really do have concerns and doubts, you could ask the doctor to refer you to the 'Second Opinion Clinic' at the National Psychosis Unit at the Maudsley Hospital in London. This is a very famous clinic and has a very good reputation. When I was working, I often referred carers there and received very good feedback. The normal approach is to be referred by your doctor. The contact details of the Clinic are:

Telephone: 020 3228 4322 or 020 3228 4276
Address: Fitzmary 2, Bethlem Royal Hospital, Monks Orchard Road Beckenham BR3 3BX. Email: slm-tr.nps@slam.nhs.uk

Professor Sir Robin Murray, who has been linked with the Psychoses Clinic for many years, kindly suggested to me that people who may feel lost and can't get help anywhere, to make direct contact with his office: robin.murray@kcl.ac.uk

Rethink Mental Illness has a very good fact sheet on second opinion, which is very comprehensive and well worth reading. Go on to Rethink Mental Illness website and search 'Second Opinion' or ring their advice line on 0300 5000 927.

Staying Involved

It is important that you stay involved at all stages of your child's treatment. Try not to be a passive observer. Many studies have shown over the years that the support of parents is crucial in helping people to stabilise and recover; indeed the importance of family involvement is enshrined in The Care Act, 2014. This act places a **duty** on the local authority to support carers.

Most healthcare staff these days recognise the importance of engaging with the family and individual carers. Part of the Care Act 2014 includes the Carer's Assessment which the health care staff have a duty to undertake. This means a health professional will sit down with you to see what help you may require. **Carer's Assessments** are particularly helpful to carers who may not have an extended family to call on or are single parents. The assessment can also look into seeing whether you are entitled to any extra funding such as the Carer's Allowance or Carer's Credit. I have met many parents over the years who did not realise they could claim for these allowances and have missed out on hundreds of pounds.

To find out about getting a Carer's Assessment and whether you are entitled to Carer's Allowance or Carer's Credit talk to your local Social Services, explain your situation and they should put you in contact with the appropriate officer. Don't delay, it could make all the difference to you and your family. If you still feel a little confused or worried about asking, then contact one of the help-lines previously mentioned, such as: Rethink Mental illness, SANE, Mind (see Chapter 9, section 3 & 4 for the addresses). I will be saying more about the Care Act and Carer's Assessment 2014 in the next chapter, because it plays a crucial role in providing support to carers/families and that is why I will repeat this message.

Chapter 9: Practical Things You Can Do to Help Matters

In this chapter we will explore in more detail some of the practical steps you and your family can take to start to get back some control of your lives and start feeling that you are heading in the right direction.

When my son had finally become a 'patient', had been allocated various health professionals to support him, and was on a course of medication, I began to feel like a passive observer. It was similar to his first day at school when I left him in the playground - he let go of my hand and disappeared through the large double doors, holding someone else's hand. I was no longer in control, and he was no longer totally dependent on us. I felt a bit like that with Steve - after months of turmoil, confusion and fear, after months of running around and ringing people, left right and centre - all of a sudden, the system had taken over - I felt a little impotent. But actually, when the system does take over, that's the time for the family to regroup, time for you to catch your breath and time to do a little planning. There are a number of simple practical things you can start to plan, that will help you move forward and give you a sense of taking back control.

1. Learn Not to Blame Yourself

One of the most important things to do when your child becomes ill is not to blame yourself because, unless you adopt the right attitude, you and your family will struggle to move forward. Having said that, there is not a parent out there who has a child with mental illness who will not at some time blame themselves in some way. Was I a bad parent? Could I have done something to have avoided this? Why didn't I spot the problem earlier? And so the search for impossible answers go on.

I have come across parents who have got themselves into a state of depression by blaming themselves. One mother, whose son had developed cannabis-induced psychosis, said to me, "My son's illness is all my fault; I should have been a better mother; I have only got myself to blame for this". It's perfectly understandable why the mother thought in this way but, when you analyse what she said, you realise that it is totally illogical because she did not cause his psychosis, she did not tell her adult child to smoke cannabis, she was not attending the college where he mixed with the young lads who were smoking cannabis and she was not to know that her son's genetic make-up tipped him more towards developing psychosis than his mates.

As Professor Fuller Torrey says in his book **Schizophrenia - A Family Manual** [56]:

> **"Developing the right attitude is the single most important thing an individual or family can do to survive schizophrenia. The right attitude evolves naturally once there is a resolution of the twin monsters of schizophrenia – blame and shame. These lie just beneath the surface of many parents, impeding the family from moving forward, souring relations among family members and threatening to explode in a frenzy of finger-pointing accusations and recriminations."**

To move forward it is essential that parents try to adopt the right attitude. Not to blame themselves or their child who did not set out to develop psychosis - it happened and no going back over history

[56] Torrey, E.F (2019) Schizophrenia - A Family Manual. 7th Edition. New York: Harper Perennial

or wringing of hands will change where you are at. Of course you can learn lessons, especially if you have younger children but, for your child who has developed cannabis-induced mental illness, don't keep looking back but look to the future and focus on getting your child well again. The chances are that they will get better and they will stabilise and go on to live a fulfilling life bringing happiness and contentment to your old age.

2. Read Up on Your Child's Diagnosis and Treatment

Whatever diagnosis your child is given, read up on it, find out about the condition, and find out about the treatment. Thanks to Sir Tim Berners Lee, the inventor of the World Wide Web, we all have access to an endless supply of knowledge. If you do not have access to the Web, then visit your local library where you can gain public access to a computer, or ask a friend or neighbour.

By using a search engine such as Google, you have the information at your fingertips. As mentioned earlier, use reliable websites such as the NHS, The Royal College of Psychiatry, the mental health charities: Rethink Mental Illness, Mind and SANE. Also, a very good US organisation is NAMH (National Association of Mental Health). Try not to get too overwhelmed with information and try and stick to reading specifically about your child's diagnosis, otherwise you can get easily sidetracked.

3. Talk to Other Parents or Join a 'Carers Group'

Meeting up with other parents and individual carers was the single most important thing we did to help my wife and me cope with our situation. When we lived in Hampshire, we discovered that the charity Rethink Mental Illness ran a small carer's group once a month in Southampton for relatives with severe mental illness, including some parents with schizophrenia. There were only about seven or eight parents attending, usually the mothers, although there were a few dads and the occasional sibling.

When I first heard the words, "Yes, my son does that as well," it was like music to my ears. And also when another member of the group said, "Yes, we did this to help alleviate the problem." It was like going to an Open University course each month. Each month we gained invaluable knowledge, knowledge we could not have gained in any other way other than through months of trial and error, making mistakes, and months of heartache.

The charity, Rethink Mental Illness, has carer groups set up all around the country. If you go into their website and type in 'carers group', there is a search page that will find the nearest group to you. If you do not have a group conveniently near to you, then Rethink will help you set one up in your town or village. It is also worth checking with your GP and with the local Mental Health services as they very often run their own carers/family groups. In some larger surgeries they will employ a generic carers worker. Rethink can be contact at:

Rethink Mental Health
89 Albert Embankment
London
SE1 7TP
Tel: 020 7840 3090

The Maudsley Hospital in London has set up a very successful 'Zoom Virtual Discussion Group' for young people with psychosis. Although it is only open to patients of the hospital, it would be worth you asking if there is a similar group in your area and, if not, then suggest they set one up. They are not complicated to establish and the benefits from such a group are immeasurable.

4. Link Up With a Specialist Charity

Don't suffer in silence or try to wrestle with problems on your own. Hopefully you should get a great deal of help from the health professionals but, if you are having problems, then, as I stated earlier, link-up with one or more of the specialist mental health charities. Rethink Mental Illness and SANE specialise in severe mental health issues. Rethink Mental Illness used to be called the 'National Schizophrenia Fellowship'; SANE, stands for 'Schizophrenia a National Emergency' - set up by the award-winning journalist and campaigner Marjorie Wallace. Both charities have helplines which can provide you with advice; this could include help with accessing benefits, carer's assessment, or help understanding the 'system'. Both have excellent fact-sheets you can download, or can be sent to you. So, there is no excuse to suffer in silence; there is a large community out there to help you and your family. If you don't have access to the internet, then either ring them or write to them - Rethink Mental Illness address is opposite:

SANE
St. Mark's Studios,
14 Chillingworth Road,
Islington,
London,
N7 8QJ
Tel: 03003047000

Other excellent charities are:

Carers UK
20 Great Dover Street
London SE1 4LX
Tel: 020 7378 4999

Mind
15-19 Broadway, Stratford,
London E15 4BQ
Tel: 020 8519 2122

5. Getting help through the Care Act 2014

The Care Act 2014 was introduced to ensure that anyone who needs care and support in the community, whether it's the elderly, physically disabled or people with mental illness, are properly assessed and this includes carers. So it is essential that you take full advantage of this act, as it could make all the difference to your family.

Arranging a Carers Assessment

I have already mentioned about the Carer's Assessment, but it is so important I will mention it again. Once your loved one has been assessed and received a treatment plan, as their carer you are entitled to a carer's assessment from the Local Authority (LA) through Social Services. The LA can provide you with support if you have 'eligible needs' which will be determined through the assessment. Support can include help if you are living alone and have specific needs that could hinder your caring role. The assessment will look to see if you have enough money to conduct your role as carer, and they could look into whether you qualify for the Carer's Allowance which is specifically designed to cushion the expense of caring. Even if you are earning and your loved one is not living with you, you may still qualify. So it is essential that you make enquires with your local social services to see if you are eligible. As previously mentioned you can always seek help from one of the many mental health charities previously mentioned: Rethink Mental Illness, SANE, Mind, to advice you. Your GP should be able to advise you where your local social services are and who to contact.

Social Care Needs Assessment for people with mental health problems

The Care Act 2014, lays out the Local Authority's **duty** to provide a 'Social Needs Assessment' to anyone who considers they have social and care needs. The legislation was introduced to help people improve their independence and wellbeing, and prevent them from deteriorating to the point where they would need additional or continuing care. It is very relevant to people with mental health problems as the Local Authority could provide extra money to help towards assisting with independence. For example, the local authority (through Social Services) could pay towards a person's leisure activities such a gym membership, or funding to attend a sheltered employment scheme.

Family or friends can apply on behalf of the individual, providing they have consent. The Needs Assessment is based on:

- What kind of health problem causes the person to need care and support?

- Whether their needs affect their ability to do certain things
- How their needs affect their day-to-day living.

If your relative is eligible, the Local Authority - through Social Services, will explore with your relative whether extra funding could help in the following areas:

- Taking more control over their life and developing independence
- Maintaining good mental health, physical health, and emotional wellbeing.
- Being safe from abuse and neglect
- Helping the individual to gain control over their day-to-day life
- Being involved in occupational, educational, training, or leisure activities
- Not being isolated
- Having enough money to live
- Maintaining good domestic, family, and personal relationships
- Having a safe and secure home

If you want to find out more about social care under the Care Act, then Rethink Mental Illness have a very good fact sheet on this, which the following QR link will lead you to.

Rethink Social Care and Eligibility fact sheet [57]

[57] (acceshttps://www.rethink.org/advice-and-information/living-with-mental-illness/treatment-and-support/social-care-assessment-under-the-care-act-2014 (accessed: 28.06.20)

6. Find out about Welfare Benefits

I don't intend to delve into the immense complexity of Welfare Benefits, but rather flag benefits up as something that you will need to grapple with. The good news is there are lots of places where you can get advice, not least the charities previously mentioned - Rethink Mental Illness, Mind, SANE and Carers UK. There are various others including, of course, Citizens Advice. You can also visit the Government's own website https://www.gov.uk/browse/benefits, which provides a comprehensive list of benefits that are available.

If you have a child under 18 with a disability (mental illness is classified as a disability), you may be entitled to claim for extra financial help, so it's important to check that out. Young people over 18 are deemed adults and are entitled to claim welfare benefits in their own right. Benefits change so it is important to check what's available with an expert at the time; currently the main welfare benefits available to people over 18 with mental illness are:

- Universal Credit
- Employment and Support Allowance (ESA)
- Personal Independence Payment (PIP)
- Attendance Allowance

Normally those over 18 should apply for benefits independently. However, if the individual is suffering with psychosis, then they are unlikely to be in any fit state of mind to run the gauntlet with the benefits system. So, they will need to have an advocate to apply to the Department of Works and Pensions (DWP) on their behalf. If they don't have a designated support worker, then normally a member of the family or close relative can apply on their behalf.

If you find yourself in the position of having to apply on behalf of your adult child, then you will first need to become 'Appointee' - this enables you to represent your adult child and talk for them. To become an Appointee with the DWP you need to complete form BF56, which you can get from: (https://www.gov.uk/become-appointee-for-someone-claiming-benefits). I became an appointee for our son; it made dealing with organisations so much easier. I should add, even if you get a support worker to apply to the DWP, it is still worth you becoming an appointee as this will enable you to talk direct to the DWP on any other issue.

For many parents this will be the first time they will have ever had to deal with the Benefits System. If this is your first time and you are applying for welfare benefits, a word of caution - it is not easy. It will take up a lot of time and you will encounter a system that is creaking at the seams. I strongly urge you to do your homework before you apply, read up on the various benefits, talk it through with one of the expert charities and, if you know a family that has gone through this process, speak with them. If you feel daunted by dealing with 'the system' then don't be afraid to ask for help.

The first place to start is your local Social Services Mental Health Team. You should be able to get the address from your local GP surgery. Ask them if they are able to provide you with specific help and they should be able to point you to a local organisation who can. Failing that, you can always contact Rethink Mental Illness, SANE, Carers UK or Mind, or your local Citizens Advice Bureau. Often you can arrange to visit them and meet with an advisor.

I certainly do not want to put you off. Indeed, it is absolutely essential that you claim for the benefits that you are entitled to. However, to emphasise why you need to do your homework and ideally get outside help and advice, the following story highlights just how difficult it can be. But it also demonstrates that, if you stick with your claim, you can succeed.

7. A Benefits Horror Story

A family had been looking after their son with schizophrenia for twenty years and he was receiving Disability Living Allowance (DLA). As his appointee, the father received a letter from the Department of Works and Pension (DWP) to say that their son's DLA was being replaced with a new benefit called Personal Independence Payment (PIP), and his son would need to be assessed for the new benefit. The family completed the assessment form and sent it off to CAPITA the private company that had the contract to undertake the PIP assessments. Three weeks later they called the family for a 40-minute interview to determine whether their son was eligible for PIP.

Four weeks following the interview, the father received a letter saying that their son had not qualified and, in fact, had failed on every one of the twenty criteria. Outraged, the father requested, under the freedom of information act, to see the assessor's full report and all the notes. Eventually, CAPITA forwarded the assessor's report which outlined their reason for declining PIP to their son. When they read the report, they were horrified at what they read as it bore no relationship to the interview that the father and his son had undertaken with CAPITA. The report stated that their son had driven to the Assessment Centre, which they claimed showed a high level of cognitive ability – their son did not even have a driving licence; the father drove. It was also claimed that their son cooked for the family, one of his hobbies was reading, and he actively socialised; all completely untrue.

Worse was to come when they discovered that the DWP had concealed a report from the GP which supported their son's level of disability, and completely contradicted the assessor's report (they were later to discover that the assessor was a General Nurse with no professional qualifications in nursing for people with mental illness). The father, along with the help of a family member who had a legal background, produced a detailed response, highlighting the many inaccuracies and false statements – within less than a month and a few red faces later, the decision was reversed, and their son was awarded PIP. The father later reported what had happened to his MP who was so shocked he sent it to the Minister.

It is understood that at least one person lost their job over it. One has to wonder whether they would have lost their job if the father had not challenged the decision! I know this story to be 100% true because it was my own son and it was me who challenged the DWP. I was able to challenge because I am reasonably articulate and I had help from someone with a legal background. The question remains; what would have happened if my son had not had a family to help him? Indeed, what happens to the thousands of severely mentally ill people who live alone, or do not have a family to fight their corner? I dread to think. Later, I found out that my case was far from unique. It seems that thousands upon thousands of people have complained about what many have called a cruel and corrupt system.

How could such a flawed and corrupt system be allowed to have been introduced? This is not some poor third world country, but the fifth richest country in the world, and one that has a reputation for looking after its citizens – the NHS being a prime example. I am sure those who introduced the changes to the benefits system did not set out to punish the disabled, did not set out to inflict poverty on society's most vulnerable citizens, but sadly that is precisely what has happened.

My hope is that by the time you have read this, the unfairness and corruption in the system will have been addressed and that, following the coronavirus upheavals, a kinder and a more humane approach to people claiming PIP and benefits generally will have prevailed – well I can at least hope.

8. Understanding How the System Works

When my son first became ill, I was completely bewildered with how the mental health services worked; it seemed like a complete maze to me. It took me quite a time to work out who was who. So, it's worth investing a little time in trying to understand what the roles are of each of the organisations and professions and how they interlink with each other. What are the various 'pathways'? How does the GP relate to the Community Mental Health Team? What is 'Primary' and 'Secondary Health Care'? What is the role of the Community Mental Health Nurse as opposed to a Mental Health Social Worker?

It will of course take time for you to get your head around the system. It certainly did for me, but once you begin to understand the roles of the different professionals and how they interrelate with each of the agencies, such as Social Services, the GP and Voluntary Organisations, you will begin to make sense of the decisions made by the professionals, and of course gain more confidence to engage with them and provide a more positive contribution.

Over the last decade, mental health services have become more integrated and work much more closely with other agencies, so the treatment and rehabilitation of individuals is much more coordinated than in previous years. This is often referred to as 'Holistic Care'. It is not going to be possible to provide a comprehensive guide to the roles of Health and Social Care staff and the general structures of Mental Health Services - that would require a book on its own - but what I can do is provide you with a 'thumbnail sketch' to get you started.

So, when your child or adult child comes in contact with a particular department or profession, whether it's a psychiatrist, Community Psychiatric Nurse or Occupational Therapist, you can ask them to explain what part of the system they are from, and how they relate to the rest of the system. Most professionals will be only too happy to explain, and always ask what you and the rest of the family can do to help. It will be appreciated. You can always go online where there is a wealth of information about the NHS Mental Health Services.

How people are treated for mental illness will depend on the severity of the condition - look at it as a spectrum; at one end there are those who are feeling a little depressed or anxious and, at the other end, there are those who have a full-blown psychosis. Most people seeking treatment will fit somewhere along that spectrum. There are two main entry levels into the Mental Health System; first level is Primary Care and the next level is Secondary Care.

Primary Care

Primary Care Services provide the first point of contact with the Healthcare System, acting as the 'front door' of the NHS. Primary Care includes your GP (General Practice), Pharmacy, Practice Nurse and School Nurse. One of the key purposes of Primary Care is to avoid hospitalisation and treat the person in the community. There are four main levels that primary care deals with when it comes to mental illness.

Level 1: This is when a person is first seen by the GP who will assess whether the person's mental health is mild enough for the person to 'self-manage' their condition, perhaps with the help of the family, or to receive 'light touch' intervention through peer support or a visit to a self-help group.

Level 2: This involves a more coordinated level of care involving the Community Mental Health Team. This could include a practice nurse or a visit from a health visitor, counsellor or psychologist to provide some therapy.

Level 3: This level comprises of higher intensity psychological therapies and/or medication for people with more complex needs such as psychosis. It will involve practitioners from more than one discipline which could include a psychiatrist, psychologist and community psychiatric nurse.

Level 4: This level comprises of specialist mental health care, including extended and intensive therapies for people with a high level of need. It is hoped the intervention of specialist mental healthcare would prevent hospitalisation.

Secondary Care

Secondary Care is usually where someone has been directly referred for more specialist help such as hospital or specialist therapy. It is when an individual's condition cannot be dealt with through Primary Care alone, such as acute psychosis, or someone is suicidal or self-harming. Once the person's condition is stabilised, they are usually referred back into the community and linked up with the Community Mental Health Team and GP for ongoing treatment and support.

When patients are discharged from hospital, they will receive a CPA or 'Care Plan Approach' which will outline how the patient's treatment will be managed in the community. It will offer help and advice about their medication, help with managing their money or any housing needs they might have, and support to try and integrate back into the community. The CPA will be coordinated by a health professional, such as a social worker, occupational therapist or community nurse.

The role of carers is very much recognised and should not be excluded from the CPA. Even if the patient has said they do not want them to be involved; carers still have a right to be listened to.

If your adult child receives a CPA, then try and ensure you get agreement with them to be involved - ideally get it written and signed by your adult child. In that way you strengthen the whole process of rehabilitation. I appreciate that some adult children will be adamant that their family should not be involved in their CPA. That is frustrating, but that doesn't mean you will be completely excluded; you can still engage with the health professionals and, although they will need to respect confidentiality, they still have a duty to engage with you, especially if your child is living with you.

Rehabilitation and Recovery

The next step is the process of rehabilitation: of course, someone with a full-blown psychosis is going to take longer than someone with milder symptoms, but the end game is the same for both - recovery! Mental health professionals tend to talk in terms of the 'Recovery Process', so you are likely to hear this frequently. In mental health, recovery may not always refer to the process of complete recovery from mental health problems in the way that we might recover from a physical health problem. Recovery can mean different things to different people. However, for many, recovery is about the realisation of goals, and the development of relationships and skills that support a positive life, with or without ongoing mental health problems [58].

Most people with mental illness do in fact recover and go on to live normal and fulfilling lives, but many live with the condition for most of their lives, but still go on to live fulfilling lives. So, whatever the prognosis is of your child, it is about working towards a stable and fulfilling life with or without psychosis, and that is exactly what my son has done, he would prefer not to have psychosis but is definitely making the very best of his life with it.

When your adult child comes out of hospital following cannabis-induced psychosis, it may seem an impossible task to get them back to anywhere near a fulfilling life - but they will; be patient and don't give up hope. It will take time and you will experience disappointments on the way, but stick with it and try and ensure you maximise the help from the mental health services.

The key components that have helped my son to stability have been:

- Getting the right medication - it may take a few goes at finding the right one
- Cognitive therapy - to help the individual gain insight and cope with their feelings, behaviour and substance misuse

[58] Mental Health Foundation

- Occupational Therapy to help give them structure and direction to their life
- Community Support Workers to help them get out and socialise and engage with the community
- Support groups, such as user networks, 'Hearing Voices Groups', and, if this is a problem, alcohol and substance misuse groups
- A loving family and supportive friends

They were and still are key components for our family. It will take time to put each piece into place and, depending on where you live, some of the components may be missing or may not fit. In that case, you just have to carry on with what you have got and maximise their particular input. It is impossible to say how long it will take; for us it was several years but then we were, for most of the time, stumbling around in the dark. If you stay active with the Community Mental Health Team and link into one of the mental health charities such as Rethink Mental Illness, SANE or Mind and, if possible join a local carer's support group, it will help to cushion the devastating impact cannabis-induced psychosis can have on you and the rest of the family. Above all, it will help seed the green shoots of hope and help you see a better future.

9. Learn to be Proactive and Not wait for the System to React

One of the biggest and quickest lessons I learnt was to be proactive and not to wait for the system to respond. It's not that mental health staff are difficult or obstructive, far from it. In most cases, mental health services lack the funding and a shortage of staff as a result of the dreadful cuts to the health service during austerity and the pressures of Covid. Seeking help from the mental health services is now a bit of a postcode lottery.

A good example of this is when our family decided to move from Hampshire to the Midlands in 2016 to live closer to my daughter. My son was receiving a lot of support from the local Mental Health Team in Southampton, including funding to attend a local sheltered employment project. When we moved, we were told that his files would be transferred and he should get continued support. This did not happen; it took me months of phone calls and emails and letters to eventually get the local Mental Health Team in Leicestershire to fully respond to my son's obvious needs. The message being that, if we had sat back and waited for the Community Mental Health Service to make contact with us, I don't think it would have happened.

Even after making contact with the CMHT, we still had to push to get my son some support. At one point I was asked, "What do you want us to do?" My response was simple; I wanted my son to have a 'Social Care Needs Assessment' which he was entitled to have under the Care Act 2014.

Once he had the assessment, the mental health team could see for themselves the level of support he needed. Eventually he was provided with a support worker and assigned a Community Psychiatric Nurse, who were both very supportive.

10. Dealing with Confidentiality

Confidentiality can be a big source of frustration for many parents when the authorities refuse to discuss your adult child's details with you. When your child reaches 18 you do not have the same level of parental control. Your child is treated as an adult and issues of confidentially kick in. If you want to talk to a health professional about your child's health then, normally, the health professional will need permission from them to share information. The way round this is to get your adult child to agree from the outset for you to act in their interest. This is known as 'giving consent' and this is what my wife and I did when my son first became ill. You simply get your child or relative to sign a statement that states they give you consent to discuss matters of confidentiality relating to their health with health staff.

If your adult child refuses to give you permission, then it is still possible for the health professionals to engage with you; indeed it is considered good practice. Unfortunately, too many organisations hide behind confidentiality: "Sorry, I am not at liberty to discuss your relatives health without their permission." This is all too often the fall-back position, so knowing your rights is crucial.

If you want more detailed information about confidentiality and disclosing information, then I recommend reading the General Medical Council (GMC) guidance to Health Care staff. It does state very clearly that carers should be involved in the patient's care and, under certain circumstances, health professionals may disclose personal information if it is of overall benefit to the patient, especially if the patient lacks capacity to give consent. This is particularly relevant to people with mental health issues. The following QR link is to the GMC guidance to health professionals. So, if you feel you are being unreasonably excluded, which sadly can happen, then reading this guidance should help you.

GMC notes on confidentiality [59]

[59] https://www.gmc-uk.org/ethical-guidance/ethical-guidance-for-doctors/confidentiality/using-and-disclosing-patient-information-for-direct-care

You can also talk to one of the Mental Health charities for advice about confidentiality - charities such as Rethink, SANE, Mind or Carers UK - if you are struggling with confidential issues regarding you and your adult child. Rethink has a very good fact sheet specifically aimed at carers, friends and relatives. See QR link below:

Rethink fact sheet: confidentiality and information for carers, friends and relatives [60]

11. Parents Learning to Live with Psychosis

Those parents who have lived with cannabis-induced psychosis for a year or more will know just how serious the illness is and the impact it has on the whole family. When we realised that our son was going to be in for the long haul, my wife felt bereaved - the little boy she had suckled, the little boy she had nurtured, was now not the boy she knew - she felt she had lost her beautiful son. In those early years I felt angry that his illness had robbed him of his youth and had threatened his future. For my wife and me it was a time of sadness and not knowing how things would end up. There were a lot of negative thoughts, sadness and despair - I feared for him, I was frightened for him and I was fearful about his future. It was clear that we now had a very seriously disabled son who could be dependent on my wife and me for the rest of our lives - had cannabis stolen our future as well as Steve's?

When a trauma such as cannabis-induced psychosis hits your

[60] https://www.rethink.org/advice-and-information/carers-hub/confidentiality-and-information-sharing-for-carers-friends-and-family/

family and the weeks turn into months and the months into years, it is natural to think of the worst and for negative thoughts to eclipse optimism and hope. It is all too easy to fall into an attitude of pessimism and despair, and allow the illness to dominate the family, casting a black shadow over everything you do. But it really does not have to be this way; indeed, it is essential that you introduce strategies to reverse this doom and gloom. OK, there may not be a cure for your child's illness - yet! But you can take action that will stop the illness causing you and your family constant sadness and gloom.

In the early part of this Chapter, I talked about practical things you can do especially at the early onset of the illness. If you and your family are a few years down the line, then I hope the following will help you to start to develop a strategy that will help you to get some of your life back. There are a few basic steps you can take and all of them are fairly common-sense things to do. None of them are complicated and all of them are doable. I will mention again some of the steps I have already discussed in this Chapter, hopefully to reinforce their importance:

1. Acceptance of the illness.

It is essential that you accept the illness for what it is. If your son or daughter has experienced the condition for a year or more, then it is very possible that the impact of the illness is going to last for some time to come. If the diagnosis is schizophrenia, then it is likely to be a long haul. There are no quick fixes with this condition which is mainly managed with a combination of medication, psychotherapy (talking therapy), social support and patience.

The sooner parents accept that they have a son or daughter who has a potential disability, the better. I often describe schizophrenia being like a stroke; like a stroke, schizophrenia is a trauma to the brain fundamentally damaging its inner workings. But, unlike a stroke where the impact of the trauma is usually very obvious to other people, schizophrenia is less visible and many of the symptoms of the trauma can be mistaken as just being lazy, not making an effort, lacking motivation, not concentrating and not listening to what people are saying. These are actually very much part of the illness, because schizophrenia affects the cognitive function of the brain, disabling the person's ability to think properly and the ability to process thought and instructions. It also affects memory.

That is why it is so easy to get frustrated with someone with schizophrenia. We certainly did in the early days because we were ignorant of just how disabling this condition was; we were expecting much more from Steve, because, on the face of it he looked a very strong and able young man, I can remember saying to him in a state of exasperation, "Steve, for heaven's sake, can't you pull yourself together and make a bloody effort?" Looking back with the benefit of hindsight, that was a cruel and crass thing to have said; the lad was frightened and bewildered at what was happening to him. It was like demanding that someone with Parkinson's Disease should make more effort to stop shaking.

To avoid yourself expecting too much from your adult child, and to stop becoming frustrated and exasperated, read up on the condition; become a 'mini' expert' on schizophrenia. It will help you become more relaxed and, above all, have more understanding and empathy with your son or daughter. It is also important that this understanding is shared with all family members! If this has struck a chord, then talk either with their Psychiatrist, Community

Psychiatric Nurse or the Mental Health Social Worker for further advice. If you struggle to accept the illness, then you will go on struggling to accept your child and the burden of care will be all the greater.

2. Getting a Family Balance

It is important to get a sense of family balance and not to allow your child's illness to dominate the family dynamics - the illness should be a part of the family, not dominating it. You and the rest of the family still have a life to live; it serves no purpose at all to live your life in 'black' as Queen Victoria did. You have to move on. Of course, the illness is not going to go away and it will remain an important part of your family's life for some time to come, but you still need to go on holiday and you still need to have fun and experience joy. I appreciate that it's hard, but you have to try and make a real effort.

When we first went on holiday abroad on our own, three or four years into Steve's illness, we racked up a huge phone bill talking to him every day-sometimes twice a day. "Mum will you ring me this afternoon to tell me you got to your hotel OK?" "Dad, did you get back from your coach ride OK?" "Mum, when are you coming home?"

Thankfully, we had family members who looked after Steve when we went away. I appreciate that's not always possible for everyone; if you are in a situation where you are unable to call on someone to 'adult mind', then talk to social services about getting respite. Respite offers carers a break from caring; it might be just for a few hours a day or longer. In some cases, carers will be offered a weekend away or a week. The NHS have very good fact-sheets on this: see QR link opposite:

NHS Respite care [61]

You will be assessed by social services to see if you are eligible. www.carersuk.org (0207 378 499) is one of many charities that could advise you about applying for respite.

3. Realistic Expectations

The one thing all parents want to know is when will their child get back to normal. With cannabis-induced psychosis/schizophrenia there is no simple answer to this question. The one thing we do know is it will take time. I once knew a mother who refused to accept that her son was really ill. That it was just a seizure that he would soon come out of. She insisted that he didn't need antipsychotic drugs and with 'God's help' he would be fine. Unfortunately, her son went from bad to worse as did the mother, who finally developed depression. Her son was sectioned and ended up in a psychiatric hospital for many months. I also knew a family who refused to discuss their son's condition, claiming that he was 'a little down' and would soon be OK to carry on with his degree and become an engineer. Sadly, that never happened and the family could never bring themselves to discuss their son who left home and disappeared into the shadows of a large city.

Most people I have come across with a diagnosis of schizophrenia adapt to their condition. They learn to live with it and manage it.

So, it is important that parents adjust their expectations in-line with limitations that the illness imposes. Of course, we must all strive for more for our loved ones; that is only natural but do it with 'realistic' expectations, and that is only achievable when you understand the conditions and the full impact they have on the individual. Reading up on the illness is essential, painful and frightening at times, but essential. Talk to Health Care staff, doctors, support workers and the Community Psychiatric Nurse who can help you in the process of coming to terms.

4. Patience

I recently asked my wife what was the single most important thing you would say to a family who are learning to live with psychosis. Chris responded immediately with, "Being patient". She went on to say:

> **"You must learn to be patient because you are inclined to gallop along expecting your loved one to keep up with you and they can't. You have to develop realistic expectations, listen to the professionals and learn from other carers. As a carer, you have to learn to walk before you can run."**

When Steve was first diagnosed, I can remember being very insistent and demanding with health professionals: "Don't you think he should have talking therapy? Shouldn't you try a different drug? Shouldn't he have occupational employment?" So the questions kept coming. Thankfully, the professionals were all mostly very 'patient' with me; they had experienced it all before - fathers like me fumbling around trying to get their child well again. Saying and trying to do whatever they believe is the right thing to do. So, my wife and I, had to learn to be patient and trust the professionals. We were very fortunate to have Professor David Kingdon as Steve's psychiatrist who was not only brilliant with Steve but managed my demands and impatience with kindness and understanding. Above all, he used to explain to me why a particular suggestion I had made was not appropriate. That investment of his time paid dividends because it helped to calm me down, and helped me to trust him and his colleagues more. This undoubtedly helped both my wife and me to work much more closely with the professionals which, in turn, very much helped Steve in the long term.

Part 5

Chapter 10: The Wider Issues of Cannabis

This Chapter will cover a range of topics that I hope will be of interest to a much wider audience than pre-teen and teenage parents for whom I initially wrote this book. My aim is to stimulate discussions and interest with the wider public, politicians, policy makers and adult cannabis users. Some of the issues I am raising in this Chapter are likely to be controversial, particularly what I consider to be the potentially huge problem of the hidden and more subtle dangers of cannabis which could be affecting hundreds of thousands of users. Other subjects I will be covering include the need to raise public awareness and health education, and the thorny discussion whether cannabis should be legalised.

The Hidden Impact of Cannabis

There is now growing evidence that psychosis could be just the tip of the iceberg with regard the impact on health of using cannabis; I am not just talking about the physical problems such as bronchitis and respiratory problems which cannabis has been linked with (The Health effects of Cannabis and Cannabinoids[62]). There is now growing evidence that cannabis can have very subtle effects on the brain. These effects, over time, can reduce an individual's ability to process information, which in turn has been linked to a range of psychosocial issues. (The person's psychological and social development.) These include:

- Poorer educational achievement
- Reduced career prospects
- Unemployment

- Increased difficulties with relationships
- Low income
- Lower level of happiness and well-being
- Delinquency
- Violence

One of the most impressive reports on this subject is by the World Health Organisation (WHO): 'The Health and Social Effects of Non-Medical Cannabis'[63]. This report pulls together many studies from around the world and provides very compelling evidence that heavy cannabis use can not only cause psychosis, but can cause a range of social, physical and mental health issues' which, for some, are irreversible. The report highlights the impact on teenagers who regularly use cannabis.

The following is an extract from the WHO report (page 25 6.1.3.1) which I thoroughly recommend reading:

> **Longitudinal studies since the 1990s have found that cannabis use before the age of 15 years predicts early school-leaving and this persists after adjustment for confounders e.g. (Ellickson et al., 1998). A meta-analysis of three Australian and New Zealand longitudinal studies (Horwood et al., 2010) confirmed this finding. Longitudinal studies have also shown that early initiation of heavy cannabis use is associated with lower income, lower college degree completion, a greater need for economic assistance, unemployment, and use of other drugs (Fergusson et al., 2016; Fergusson & Boden, 2008.**

Another useful study by Brook J.S. (et al) on 'Marijuana Use

---

[63] https://www.who.int/substance_abuse/publications/cannabis_report/en/index11.html (accessed 23/9/20)

Beginning in Adolescence'[64] highlights a range of adverse effects on young teenagers which has a lasting effect into adulthood. The outcomes highlighted in the study include lower physical and psychological well-being, less success at work, increased difficulty with relationships and lack of motivation to 'follow through on occupational goals'. It is important to stress that these negative impacts of cannabis generally refer to regular users of cannabis; for example, teenagers who use cannabis more the 20 times before they are 17, or are 'chronic to moderate users'. As with most studies on the subject, the younger the person takes cannabis, and the regularity and potency of the cannabis, often determines the long-term health and psychosocial outcomes.

The numbers affected by the hidden impact of cannabis could far exceed those who are treated for cannabis-induced psychosis (between 7,500 to 10,000 each year). Studies on the numbers of those affected by the psychosocial impact are still in their infancy - as was the research into tobacco use in the 1950s. However, looking at recent studies and talking to experts, and from my own observations of older cannabis users, the numbers affected by the psychosocial impact of cannabis use could be in the hundreds of thousands, especially if you include parents, friends and work colleagues. I don't consider this statement widely exaggerated if you consider the 2.6 million people in the UK who use cannabis, and the new generation of users constantly coming on stream who are using the more potent blends of cannabis.

So, based on the psychosocial studies that currently exist, and the evidence we have on cannabis-induced psychosis, it does not take a lot of working out that the real impact cannabis is having on people's health and well-being could be far greater than we have been led to believe. I accept that no one fully knows the true figure

---

[64] Brook.J.S., et.al (2013) Adult Work Commitment, Financial Stability, and Social Environment as Related to Trajectories of Marijuana Use Beginning in Adolescence found in: https://www.ncbi.nlm.nih.gov/pmc/articles/PMC3711606/ (accessed:28.06.20)

yet, and more research is desperately needed.

But the signs are that the real negative impact of cannabis is potentially a huge problem. I am convinced that when the research has been conducted, it will reveal an enormous social and financial burden to society, and will shock a lot of regular cannabis users as it did cigarette smokers seventy years ago. If we are going to get on top of this situation, users of cannabis should try to be upfront and honest, and warn teenagers of the potential dangers of taking cannabis at such a young age. People who continue to deny the dangers are sending the wrong message to young people, and reinforce a false and dangerous message.

Cannabis - Violence and Knife Crime

Could a plant associated with flower power, feeling mellow and having the giggles, really be linked to violence and knife crime? Well, sadly the answer is yes. There is a growing body of evidence that is now firmly linking cannabis with violence and even murder - I can almost hear the cries of outrage from the supporters of cannabis; "Blaming it for mental health issues is bad enough but blaming cannabis for murder is too much." Well, before I provoke too much hostility, let me explain.

A useful comparison is alcohol; the link between alcohol and violence is well documented and well understood by most people. In 2018 the Crime Survey of England and Wales, the police reported 218,790 alcohol-related violent incidents. In the same way people become intoxicated with alcohol, people become intoxicated with cannabis. Both cause the individual to lose control of their senses, both cause the individual to become less inhibited, and both substances can cause unpleasant side effects, including anger, frustration and violence, albeit on a lesser scale with cannabis because fewer people use it.

Publicly, there has been very little said about cannabis and violence even though there have been many studies around the world making the link, especially with crime and delinquent behaviour generally. The many studies that have taken place appear to have fallen under the radar of governments around the world, including the UK.

There is little doubt in my mind that the supporters of cannabis have done a superb job over the years in maintaining the gentle, harmless, relaxing image of cannabis, when in fact recorded studies of a link with crime and violence are well documented and go back many years.

In 1997, academics Fergusson and Horwood looked at delinquency of sixteen-year-olds in New Zealand, and found a link with violent behaviour and cannabis use. The same pattern was established in a follow-up study when the individuals reached the age of 21 (Fergusson et al. 2002a).

In 2000 a longitudinal study of mental disorder and violence, followed 961 New Zealand youths from birth. This study found a link with 7.6% of youths who self-reported they had engaged in violence, and had been using cannabis (Arseneault et al). Studies in the United States, England and Australia in 1999, found that approximately 60% of arrestees for criminal activity tested positive for cannabis (Pacula and Kilmer at el).

It is important to stress that a lot of these early studies did not prove that cannabis caused violent behaviour because the researchers had to take into account many other factors - those who took part in the studies also consumed alcohol and other drugs. Some were involved in delinquency before they took cannabis; they came from dysfunctional families where deviant behaviour was more the norm. But what these early studies were showing was a 'link'. Cannabis was regularly being cited as being present when criminal and deviant behaviour took place. As the research became more sophisticated over the years, and social scientists and neuroscientists have studied the impact of cannabis in more depth; the link between violence and violent behaviour is becoming more apparent.

The award-winning writer and Journalist, Alex Berenson's meticulously written book, **'Tell Your Children - The Truth About Marijuana, Mental Illness and Violence'**. (Free press 2019) brings the subject more up to date with what Berenson calls the 'hidden epidemic' of violence linked to cannabis. The book provides extensive personal stories backed up by studies. Berenson also looked into a number of court cases involving violent crimes that had taken place in the US. He discovered that in some horrific mass killings the perpetrators had been using cannabis prior to their crimes. When he looked more closely into the cases, another clear link started to emerge; many of the assailants were also suffering with psychosis/schizophrenia. Was this just a coincidence or was the combination of cannabis and psychosis proving to be a lethal combination?

Berenson cites the tragic case of a mother who stabbed all of her eight children and one niece to death. It became one of the first judicial findings where the judge linked the murders with cannabis use, schizophrenia and violence. As Berenson points out, the link made by the judge – that cannabis was a contributory cause – is a connection that cannabis advocates are desperate to hide.

Berenson goes on to cite numerous studies (page 167) including a 2013 paper in **'The Journal of Interpersonal Violence'**. Using Federal data of 12,400 American high school students, the study – **'Does Heavy Adolescent Marijuana Lead to Criminal Involvement in Adulthood'** by Green, Doherty and Ensminger - examines the link between alcohol, marijuana, and aggression. The researchers' initial hypothesis, which they published as part of the paper, was that alcohol increased violence, while marijuana reduced it. Instead, they found that students who had recently used marijuana – but not alcohol – were more than three times as likely to be physically aggressive as those who abstained from both, even after adjusting for race and gender. Those who used alcohol, not marijuana, were 2.7 times as likely and those who use both were almost six times as likely to be physically aggressive.

A 2016 paper in **'Psychological Medicine'**[65] examined marijuana use and criminal behaviour among 400 boys in London who were followed up for more than 40 years, beginning in 1961. Their marijuana use was surveyed when they were 18, 32 and 48. The paper found marijuana use at all three periods was associated with a nine-fold increase in violent behaviour, even after adjusting the other variables. Berenson points out that the first four states to legalise marijuana for recreational use - Colorado, Washington, Alaska, Oregon – have all experienced large increases in aggravated assaults and murders since legalisation.
Berenson adds that one of the key links between cannabis and violence is psychosis and, if you include other associated factors such as depression and anxiety - all associated with cannabis - we can begin to see the link between cannabis and violent behaviour is clearer. If you add in those young people who are from dysfunctional families, excluded from school, unemployed, rejected by their peers and associating with others with deviant

---

[65] Schoeler, T., (et.al) "Continuity of cannabis use and violent offending over the life course" Psychological Medicine Vol.46. issue 8. June 2016.pp.1663-1677

behaviour, then the link with violent behaviour becomes even clearer.

The link between knife crime and cannabis is even more complex, but complexity should not be a reason to deter putting forward sensible arguments supporting the link.

According to the Office of National Statistics report: **'Crime in England and Wales: year ending December 2019'**, there were 45,627 offences in the UK involving knives or sharp instruments recorded by police; a 7% rise year on year, and 49% higher than 2011.

The Mayor of London, Sadiq Khan recently admitted that knife crime keeps him awake at night, with fatal stabbings of teenagers in the capital rising to their highest level in over a decade. Clearly, cannabis cannot be blamed for all these crimes but, in my view and based on the evidence we have on the link between cannabis and violence, I am convinced there must also be a link with knife crime.

Making this link does not mean we should discount legalising cannabis or demonising it; making the link is legitimising a discussion about how we, as a society, should approach knife crime. We now have a wealth of evidence linking cannabis with mental illness as discussed earlier. We also have considerable evidence linking cannabis with crime and violent behaviour; so, it doesn't take a lot of working out that knife crime could also be linked to these trends.

I am convinced that the link can be found when we look at the very high levels of THC now found in most street cannabis. The NHS's own figures show that the potency of cannabis has more than doubled over the last 20 years and trebled if you go back to the 1960s. This correlates with the increase in numbers of recorded cannabis-induced cases of psychosis and other health issues. It is when we look at the link with cannabis and our mental health, and how cannabis can alter the functioning of the brain, that we can begin to fully understand the impact cannabis can have on mental health, aggression, violence and knife crime. The academic magazine – **'Psychological Medicine '(Cambridge Press) Vol 46 issue 8 June 2016 pp 1663- (Continuity of Cannabis Use and Violent Offending Over the Life Course).** The study suggests that impairments in neurological circuits controlling behaviour may underlie impulsive, violent behaviour. It concludes that, as a result of cannabis altering the normal neural functioning in the ventrolateral pre-frontal cortex, **'persistent use of cannabis may cause violent behaviour as a result of changes in brain function due to smoking over many years'.**

It concludes:

> **Together, these results provide strong indication that cannabis use predicts subsequent violent offending, suggesting a possible causal effect, and provide empirical evidence that may have implications for public policy.**

So, putting together the toxic mixture of psychosis, depression, lost in the school system, unemployment, dysfunctional parents, poor housing, tough neighbourhoods, gang culture and high potency cannabis, it should be no surprise that cannabis can give rise to violence and knife crime. If society is to deal with knife crime, then it is essential that cannabis is included in any future plans to try and reduce this dreadful epidemic.

The Cost of Mental Illness

Mental illness is not only a dreadful burden to the individual, it is also a huge burden on society as a whole. According to the Department of Health's own report **'No Health Without Mental Health'**[66], published in Feb 2011, mental illness is the single largest cause of disability in the UK, contributing up to 22.8% of the total disease burden, compared to 15.9% for cancer and 16.2% for cardiovascular disease. The wider economic costs of mental illness in England have been estimated at £105.2 billion each year. I'll say that again, £105.2 billion each year. That is more than twice the UK's Defence Budget (£41.3 billion for 20/21) and larger than the education budget (£93 billion in 2019). The huge cost of mental illness includes the economic and social costs - the costs of Health and Social Care, benefits, lost productivity at work.

These are staggering figures which just roll off the tongue, but the disgraceful thing about the huge cost of mental illness is that it is one of the few chronic conditions which can be reversed and, indeed, most people with mental illness can be treated, even with conditions such as schizophrenia. The vast majority who experience mental illness can and do return to a normal life. Studies show that health education and early intervention not only help to improve people's well-being, it can also save society billions of pounds. **'The Journal of Epidemiological and Community Health (vol 71, issue 8),** reported that, for every £1 spent on public health £14 will be subsequently returned to the wider society and social care economy. We all have a responsibility to ensure that our hard-earned taxes are used to the greatest effect, and not accept the government's cutting of health programmes that would otherwise substantially improve the quality of life for our fellow citizens and, at the same time, save billions for the tax payer.

The Need to Raise Public Awareness

We now know that cannabis can be extremely dangerous to young teenagers with increasing numbers being admitted to mental health units. The key question is how do we get the message across? How do we get parents to understand the difference between THC and CBD? How do we make them aware that the potency of cannabis saturating the illegal market is highly dangerous and can cause brain damage? Are parents aware that 30% of all new admissions for psychosis in parts of London are linked to cannabis use? The answer to these questions is likely to be a resounding No! Certainly, the many parents I have come in contact with during the course of writing this book have not been aware of just how dangerous the new strands of cannabis are.

It is clear, in my view, that a major public health campaign needs to take place. Yes, there are campaigns going on, but they are only scratching the surface. If these were being successful then cannabis use would not be increasing amongst teenagers. It is essential that future campaigns are planned and continue until such time the incidence of cannabis-induced psychosis has drastically reduced.

We know public awareness campaign can work, following the 'Tell Frank' campaign mentioned earlier, if they are funded and sustained correctly. It was in 2003 that the then Labour government launched the successful drugs awareness campaign 'Talk to Frank' (www.talktofrank.com). It was, in my view, a very important component in helping to reduce the numbers of people using cannabis – see the graph below. Cannabis peaked in the late 1990s and then started to dramatically decline. This directly coincided with the huge increase in media coverage at that time which the National Charity Rethink Mental Illness orchestrated with the help of 'The Times.'

As you can see from the graph below (taken from the Home Office statistics bulletin 14/18 July 2018), the impact of the campaign and the news coverage was impressive. I should point out that there may have been other factors that could have contributed to the decline such as users turning to other forms of illicit drugs. But all the same, the increased media and government coverage unquestionably had real impact. You will note that the decline in cannabis use started to flatten and then started to reverse around 2012, precisely at the time the government's austerity cuts started to bite. In 2013 the government cut the marketing budget of 'Talk to Frank' and, although the website is still there, it meant the campaign had no real voice. Cutting the marketing budget is like telling the Rolling Stones to substantially reduce the volume at their concerts to save electricity. If you are serious about getting your message across, the last thing you do is to cut your marketing budget.

Figure 7: Reported Proportion of Adults Using Cannabis, 1996-2018, Age groups 16-24 &16-15

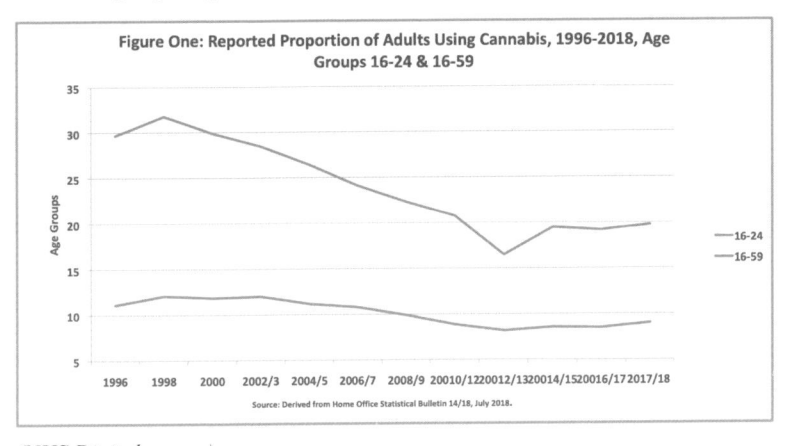

(NHS Digital survey)

Pepsi still spend billions on marketing, but just dropping their marketing budget by 5% would cost billions in sales - why don't governments understand this?

When it comes to marketing the health and wellbeing of the nation, marketing should be an absolute priority. It is foolish in my view; just think how many more young people could have been diverted from using cannabis from 2012 onwards had the campaign continued to receive the funding it needed. This foolish and short-sighted decision may well have led to hundreds of new cases of young people developing cannabis-induced mental illness which will cost us taxpayers dearly in the future

It is not just the extra cost to the Health and Social Care budget of having to support people with a psychotic condition, but the loss in tax revenue to the government because individuals are unable to work and contribute tax to society. For some that loss in tax revenue will continue for the rest of their lives. Cannabis-induced mental illness is a huge burden on the welfare state. These often highly disabled individuals will require welfare benefits, social support, housing and highly expensive medication - often for decades. Then, to top it all, is the hidden cost to the family - the impact on their health - days lost at work sorting out endless mini-crises, bailing their loved one out of financial messes, and so on. All for the sake of making the Treasury feel good, by making ill-informed cuts to social care.

The Role the Education System has to Play

The education system can't do everything, but it can do more to steer children away from using cannabis and drugs generally. I have spoken to a number of educationalists, all of whom agreed that schools and colleges could go a lot further to stem the growth of cannabis amongst young people - if they were given the resources.

Many of the young people who go on to become regular users of cannabis are often ones that have been excluded by the education system [67]. They have so often been cut loose and allowed to drift away from school, and end up with other like-minded youngsters where drug use, delinquent behaviour and gang culture is more the norm; a place where they begin to have a sense of belonging and where they are out of sight and out of mind from the education system! Drug dealers are targeting these kids and recruiting them [68]. One teacher stated that schoolchildren who have been excluded can earn £400 a week as a 'runner' for a drug dealer. Why would they want to go back to school where they don't feel they belong. Reaching out to these young people, and stopping them from drifting away from the main-stream of society, is absolutely essential, if we, as a society, are serious about tackling the current level of delinquent behaviour and, in particular, cannabis and drug use.

According to research commissioned by the Home Office, about children who had been permanently excluded from school, numerous young people in their study suffered from:

> **pervasive social and educational disadvantage. This included child sexual abuse, frequent shifts between homes, parental violence, bereavement and homelessness. Eighteen per cent of the youngsters in our survey had been 'looked after' by local authorities, 47 per cent were entitled to free school meals, a key indicator of social deprivation, 45 per cent were known to Social Services and 20 per cent to Youth Justice**

---

[67] Truancy School Exclusion and Substance Misuse: Lesley McAra, University of Edinburg 2014
[68] Rise in school Exclusion linked to Souring Numbers Recruited by County dealers: David Cohen 6 Jan 2020

(now replaced by Youth Offending Teams). Eight of the 28 interviewees had spent time in Young Offender Institutions.

Many children who are excluded also experience serious mental health problems which can occur before and after being excluded [69]. These children need our help, not rejection which many of them have experienced most of their lives. As a civilised society we have an absolute responsibility to rescue as many of these children as possible. It can and must be done!

It only took me an afternoon surfing the net to discover that there is considerable research showing if schools are given the resources and training many of the children roaming shopping centres, following being kicked out of school, could successfully return. Indeed, if schools adopted the right strategies, they could avoid these children being kicked out in the first place.

A paper by the Kings Fund[70] points out how investing in Health Education and giving time to young people to learn about life skills, problem solving, building self-esteem, teenage pregnancy and substance abuse, can alter children's behaviour, especially those children at risk.

Another excellent document by the Department for Education (DFE) provides a host of examples of good practice, and cites numerous research papers which tackle alternatives to exclusion [71].

So, whilst the answers are out there, according to many teachers and educationalists I spoke to, schools have not had the resources to implement the strategies to provide effective intervention.

69   Poor Mental Health 'Both Cause and Effect of School Exclusion, University of Exeter, 2020
70   The Kings Fund, Healthy Living
71   Social Exclusion: A Literature Review on Continued Disproportionate Exclusion of Certain Children

One educationalist told me:
> "It is so frustrating when I go into a school to advise them about a particular child that needs support, only to find out later that the child received a few weeks extra help when they needed at least six months. It's like giving a patient with cancer two sessions of chemotherapy when they need six. It is fundamentally wrong."

She went on to say that she did not blame the schools, because they are having to wrestle with budgets. However, some schools are guilty of playing the game of dumping 'difficult children' onto another school, which says more about keeping up the image of the school that rescuing the child.

As an outsider I find it incredible that children are still being excluded and in fact the levels are increasing. The official figures from the Government show just under 8000 children being excluded each year. In a report by David Cohen in the Evening Standard, he claims the figure could be twice that, at 16000 children each year [72].

There is some good news, I am pleased to say, which may help to reverse things somewhat. Finally, the government have decided to reverse the decision of personal skills training known as PSHE (Personal Social Health Education) from advisory to mandatory. From September 2020, it became **compulsory** for schools to teach children about good physical and mental health, how to stay safe on and offline, and the importance of healthy relationships.

Whether schools will get the resources they need to adopt the good practice identified by the DFE – dedicated teachers trained in PSHE, pastoral support, training programmes for all staff, actively engaging and supporting parents, etc. - is to be seen.

---

[72] Numbers of Pupils Excluded From School could be more than double the official figures

To Legalise or Not To Legalise?

With countries around the world relaxing their laws on cannabis, and big business snapping at the heels of governments to legalise, the pressure is on for more countries to liberalise their laws on the recreational use of cannabis, not least the UK. Many countries have already legalised cannabis for medical use, including the UK (2018). But only a handful of countries have made it legal nationwide: Uruguay, Canada, Georgia, South Africa and several states in the US; Luxembourg looks set to be the first European country to fully legalise cannabis in 2021. I should point out that many countries, such as Holland, Portugal, Spain and Germany, took a more liberal approach to cannabis many years before Uruguay legalised cannabis. However, cannabis still remains illegal in these counties who simply 'relaxed' their laws; for example, making possession a civil offence - like illegal parking or speeding- rather than a criminal offence. In Holland the official tourist website is quick to point out that cannabis is still illegal. On the face of it, the question to legalise or not to legalise does seem a fairly straightforward one. For supporters of cannabis, legalising is about giving people freedom of choice without being criminalised and also taking it out of the hands of criminal gangs. For those who are against, legalising is a Public Health issue; it's a dangerous substance which can cause serious harm to people.

When you start to dig deeper into both sides of the argument, it becomes far less straightforward. There are powerful arguments on both sides. When I started writing this book, I supported the legalisation of drugs, even though my own son became a casualty. Six months into writing my book I began to realise just how complicated legalisation is. I began to realise that legalisation is not just about freedom of choice and protecting society from criminal gangs, but also about protecting people's health, particularly young people, who often look at the world in simplistic black and white terms. Legalising cannabis would, without doubt, send the wrong message to teenagers who would interpret legalisation as the thumbs up from us adults. It's a very difficult circle to try and square, but it's one we must if we are to move forward and leave a legacy for future generations of which we can be proud, and one that future historians can look back and say, "they finally got it right". I hope that the following chapter will help in some small way to move us in that direction.

Before we go into a detailed discussion, it is important to understand the various levels of 'legalisation and prohibition'.

The following is a very brief overview:

1. Complete prohibition - Exists in countries such as Japan, Iceland, Russia and Hungary. If you are caught, it could mean a custodial sentence for those who supply and use cannabis, even if it is for medical purposes. There are still a number of countries who impose the death sentence and carry them out, such as China, Singapore and Saudi Arabia, but these are targeted at those who supply or traffic illegal drugs.

2. Partial Prohibition - Often referred to as 'decriminalisation', which means that it is still a criminal offence to supply but a lesser offence if you use it. It can vary enormously from country to country; however, most countries focus on criminalising those who supply, but a civil offence if you use it. You do not get a criminal record, just a fine or warning. Portugal became the first country in the world in 2001 to treat drug users as sick people, instead of criminals. However, you can be arrested or made to go into rehab if caught several times in possession. Portugal's policy rests on three pillars: one, that there's no such thing as a soft or hard drug, only healthy and unhealthy relationships with drugs. Two, that an individual's unhealthy relationship with drugs often conceals social and personal issues, and three, that the eradication of all drugs is an impossible goal. Many hold Portugal as a beacon of drug reform.

Partial permission can also include the use of specialist cannabis extracts for medical use and the sale of cannabis oils. Many countries around the world have decriminalised cannabis for medical use, but it still remains a criminal offence for recreational use.

3. Legalisation - usually means that it is legal for recreational use, but you must have a licence to sell it. Canada, for example, has taken on state control of the production, possession, distribution and sale of cannabis. It is still an offence to drive under the influence of cannabis as it is with alcohol, and anyone selling to people under 18 can be imprisoned for up to 14 years. The level of THC is strictly limited. If you would like to know more about the cannabis laws in Canada, then visit the official Canadian Government website:

Cannabis laws and regulations in Canada[73]

https://www.canada.ca/en/health-canada/services/drugs-medication/cannabis/laws-regulations.html (accessed;29.06.20)

In Uruguay, you are only able to access cannabis if you register with the state. You are allowed to either grow up to four plants at home for your own use, join a cannabis 'Growers Club' which produces cannabis for its members, or purchase it from an approved pharmacy. Uruguay still has strict laws with regards to selling it illegally.

In the US it is still a Federal offence to use cannabis for recreational use, but individual States have the power to make their own laws; those that have, strictly regulated the sale and distribution.

Legalising for Medical Use.

This has been one of the fastest areas of development, with countries around the world legalising cannabis for medical use, including the UK as I have already mentioned. Cannabis extracts are now freely available on the internet, manufactured by some of the world's leading pharmaceutical companies. Market analyst (www.market.businessinsider.com) reported that recent marijuana product sales in the US are already worth **52 billion** dollars per annum. Recently, Colorado generated 35 million dollars in tax revenue. Currently investment is being channelled into cannabis research and development. It has recently been reported in **The Guardian** 2/3/2019), that the European cannabis market could be worth £106 billion by 2028 [74]. The Prohibition Partner's investment company also reported that the UK market could be worth £2.31 billion by 2024 [75]. Even though these estimates could be a little optimistic, it is clear which way we are heading.

A point of warning: claims made by some manufacturers about cannabis products are very suspect and have been dismissed by many scientists. The research I mentioned earlier, published by the

---

[74] https://www.theguardian.com/business/2019/mar/02/legal-medicinal-recreational-cannabis-industry-investors (accessed: 30.06.20)

[75] Loc.cit

US National Academy in Chapter 4, provides an excellent critique of the therapeutic effects of cannabis and, while supporting some claims, dismisses many others. So be warned, don't fall for the hype, do your research first. The BBC has a good online article about this issue with links to research from Nottingham University to back it up (https://www.bbc.co.uk/news/health-48950483).

There is also some very useful information on the NHS website:

Cannabis based products for medical use[76]

Another word of caution: because the cannabis laws vary so much from country to country and even within countries such as the US, it is essential to check first what the law is before you think of using cannabis abroad.

The Case to Legalise Cannabis for Recreational Use

Support to legalise cannabis for recreational use in the UK has been around for decades. It mostly started in the 60's during the 'Flower Power' years. Numerous action groups sprang up lobbying governments to legalise and relax the laws. The main arguments by these groups are:

---

76   https://www.england.nhs.uk/medicines-2/support-for-prescribers/cannabis-based-products-for-medicinal-use/cannabis-based-products-for-medicinal-use-frequently-asked-questions/?fbclid=IwAR37jPO3cCBVBJx14_iR-l_-l680N__kqgOJqzWc5yLZfLfZV8fZ2zrUKKk#who-can-prescribe-a-cannabis-based-product-for-medicinal-use

1. Millions enjoy cannabis and it's a relatively harmless plant which 2.6 million people enjoy in the same way as people enjoy alcohol, smoking and coffee. It helps people to chill out and relax.
2. Supporters argue that cannabis is safer than alcohol which is linked to 358,000 hospital admissions in 2018 according to NHS digital, and the numbers who are adversely affected by cannabis are tiny compared to alcohol.
3. Prohibition does not work: the high numbers of people using cannabis demonstrates that prohibition is not working.
4. It takes it out of the hands of criminals: by legalising cannabis, it is argued that it will shift the production and sale of cannabis away from the hands of criminals.
5. Legalisation will provide the government with much - needed revenue in the form of taxable income.
6. Legalising would substantially reduce the cost of policing cannabis and the cost to the judicial system.
7. It will provide an opportunity for the government to regulate the strength of cannabis by reducing the dangerous levels of THC which has been deliberately increased over the years by criminal gangs.
8. What is the point of having a law which can easily be broken and brings the law into disrepute? In a study by Tittle and Rowe in 1974 they showed that if a law is going to be effective, there needs to be at least a 30% chance of being apprehended; for cannabis, the chance of being caught using is .01% (Lenton, 2000).
9. One of the leading arguments by supporters is freedom of choice. It is argued that citizens should be able to make their own choice in the same way as people choose

whether to drink alcohol, which can also be dangerous and addictive.
10. Supporters argue that public opinion is growing to legalise cannabis with 47% in support of relaxing the cannabis laws.
11. Cannabis has been used for centuries to treat a range of health conditions, and research shows it does help with pain.

It is worth saying something about the police and their position on cannabis. Off the record many in the police force believe that cannabis should be decriminalised. One former journalist told me that when the government considered moving cannabis from a Class C drug, back to a Class B, the police actively lobbied the then Home Secretary, Charles Clark MP, to keep cannabis as a Class C drug. As we now know this failed, as cannabis was moved to a Class B drug in 2008, which it remains today. The reason the police are keen to decimalise cannabis is because many in the police force consider that cannabis takes up too much police time and, as mentioned in point 6 above, it would reduce the cost of policing cannabis and the cost to the judicial system.

The Case Against Legalising for Recreational Use

1. The evidence that cannabis is linked to long-term psychosis and schizophrenia is now conclusive. Even many advocates of cannabis agree that there is a risk. Therefore, it is argued, it is wrong to condone a substance that we know can damage the brains of young people.
2. There is a fear that legalisation will send completely the wrong message to young people. We adults will in

effect be telling teenagers that it's OK to use because the government is allowing its use.
3. Teenagers are most at risk of severe mental health problems as a result of smoking cannabis; legalising could encourage young people to use it more, and increasing the numbers of young people developing schizophrenia.
4. Even though most people who smoke cannabis do not develop psychosis, that shouldn't mean that the thousands who do develop severe mental illness be considered dispensable, and treated as collateral damage for the sake of people who want to use it.
5. There are increasing studies showing that cannabis can have very subtle and long-term effects on people's cognitive functioning, and the numbers could be in the tens or even hundreds of thousands.
6. Cannabis can reduce students' academic performance leading to poorer exam results and even dropping out of school and college. This in turn can affect people's career prospects, earning less than their peers who don't use cannabis. It can affect people's ability to form long-term relationships and is associated with a more unstable and chaotic lifestyle.
7. People can become addicted to cannabis. It can lead to harder drugs, disrupted lives, poverty and violence.
8. If cannabis is commercialised, there is a likelihood that big business will be driven by profit and not people's public health. There is concern they will target sales to the biggest users.
9. The revenue gains legalisation could offer could be wiped out by the Public Health costs of treating and supporting individuals and their parents affected by

cannabis-induced mental illness. Some argue that the social and economic costs of legalising cannabis would be far greater than tax revenues.
10. Cannabis can cause lung disease and heart problems. It has also been linked to certain cancers and can affect the fertility of woman.
11. Minimal health benefits - The medical benefits of cannabis are overstated. International research shows only a small number of physical conditions have some positive results and the vast majority of claims have little scientific backing.

There is no doubt that there are powerful arguments on both sides of the cannabis debate. On the 'pros' side, I am particularly impressed with the argument that prohibition has not stopped the 2.6 million people currently using it, and the argument that legalising would take it out of the hands of criminals. On the 'cons' side, I am impressed with the argument that it would send the wrong message to young people, and it would be wrong to condone something which we know can cause damage to young people's brains.

To help develop the debate on this very controversial subject, where better to look than those countries that have already legalised cannabis for recreational and medical use. These countries have created a mass human experiment with cannabis which offers the rest of the world an opportunity to observe and, hopefully, learn from their experiences. Some studies have already taken place in a number of these countries and, although it is still early days, they do show some very important trends.

What the Recent Studies Show.

In October 2019, **'The Lancet'** published a paper: **'Public health implications of legalising the production and sale of cannabis for medical and recreational use'**. This paper is very comprehensive. It looks at various studies that have taken place in countries that have legalised cannabis around the world. The paper does point out that legalisation is at an early stage but, all the same, it reports on some very important findings.

One of the key findings is that adult use of cannabis appears to have increased since legalisation. Adolescent use has stayed much the same, although one worrying trend shows that the 'perceived' risk of cannabis for people under 21 has reduced. This backs up the concerns of those who said that legalising cannabis would send the wrong message to teenagers. The paper also reports on surveys that show that some individuals are reporting increased symptoms of dependency and mental illness. In some US states, road crash fatalities linked to high levels of THC have increased after legalisation.

The US **'Journal of Addiction'**, published a study in February 2016 entitled; **'What we know about the impact of laws related to marijuana'** by Maxwell & Mendleson. It reported on post-legalisation in Denver and Seattle cities that legalised cannabis in 2012. What they found was an increase in hospital admission to emergency departments, and calls for help to drug centres related to cannabis following legalisation. They also reported that cannabis related arrests were down, but an increase in the level of illegal trafficking of cannabis between US states.

Oregon legalised cannabis in 2014. A report by the Oregon Health Authority in 2016: **'Marijuana attitudes and health effects in Oregon'** reported that more youths in Oregon use cannabis than smoke tobacco. That 1-10 eighth grade, (12 to 13 year olds), and 1 in 5 (19%) eleventh grades (15 to 16 year olds). So is it any wonder that calls from teenagers to helplines have increased?

Another revealing report from Oregon Health Authority: **'Oregon medical marijuana program operations and compliance assessment May 2018'.** The report highlights: 'insufficient funding and staffing resources to meet the demands of robust regulation' and 'Inspection did not keep pace with applications'.

Looking through a few blogs, cannabis users are still using the 'illegal market' because it was stronger and more potent than the legal products, and also there was not enough 'legal' outlets to obtain cannabis. This is something that users in other countries who have legalised cannabis have complained about.

Another useful paper, published by the Society for the Study of Addiction: **'Evaluating the public health impacts of legalising recreational cannabis use in the United States'** by W Hall and M Lynskey, appears to back up concerns raised in other studies. The report found that:

> Legalisation of recreational use of marijuana will probably increase in the long term, but the magnitude and timing of any increase is uncertain. It will be critical to monitor: cannabis use in household and high school surveys; cannabis sales; the number of cannabis plants legally produced; and the tetrahydrocannabinol (THC) content of

cannabis. Indicators of cannabis-related harms that should be monitored include car crash fatalities and injuries; emergency department presentations; presentations to addiction treatment services; and the prevalence of regular cannabis use among young people in mental health services and the criminal justice system [77].

This report is important as it highlights the need to monitor the legislation which is going to require substantial investment by legislators, which I will discuss later.

The way cannabis is supplied in countries that have legalised is fast developing into a major issue, and is presenting some real challenges to legislators. Transform - Drugs and policy Foundation - a charity based in Bristol in the UK, made some very interesting observations in their report: **'Cannabis Legalisation In Canada - One Year On'**. The report points out that the Canadian approach has been criticised for creating barriers to entry for smaller enterprises, because of the requirement of major production investment before they can obtain a licence, thereby favouring the larger corporate companies who now dominate the market. The report goes on to highlight how large investment organisations are moving into the cannabis market in other parts of the world:

> **Further afield, the emergence of multi-billion-dollar cannabis corporations has led to accusations of predatory activities in emerging cannabis markets in low and middle income countries. In Colombia, for example, Canadian companies currently represent 85% of total investment in the emerging medical cannabis market. Local farmers have expressed concerns about both environmental impacts marginalised from decision

[77] https://onlinelibrary.wiley.com/doi/abs/10.1111/add.13428 (accessed:30.06.20)

making. Canadian venture capital has been similarly prominent in emerging cannabis markets in Mexico, Jamaica, Lesotho and elsewhere.

I fear that the good intention of legislators to liberalise and control the supply and use of drugs, such as cannabis, could be undermined by the single-minded greed of some Corporations and Venture Capitalists.

Summary - Legalisation of Cannabis

Although it is early days, and more time is needed to get accurate data, it does appear from the preliminary studies that legalisation has led to an increase in the use of cannabis amongst adults, and there are signs that more people are seeking help for cannabis dependency and mental health issues. Young people don't appear to have increased their use. However the 'perceived risk' of using cannabis has reduced. There are also reports of increasing numbers of young people seeking help for health issues following legalisation. More research needs to be done, but there is little doubt in my mind that the legalisation does appear to have sent the wrong message to young people - the very group who are most at risk, and the very group society is keen to protect.

Legalisation has clearly reduced the opportunity for criminal gangs to sell their product, which is a major plus. However, criminal gangs have not gone away. Criminals will look elsewhere to sell their illegal drugs and will have no compunction about targeting under-age teenagers. Criminals are also likely to entice adults with higher levels of THC - something which is currently restricted in legal markets.

There are early indications in the USA that those who have the responsibility for enforcing the regulations are poorly resourced with not enough funding and staff. If this trend is followed in other countries, it will be open season for the less ethical and socially responsible commercial companies. Concerns have already been raised in Canada regarding the 'predatory' activities of Venture Capitalists as they pour billions and billions of dollars into this emerging market around the world. **The power of wealth could corrupt and distort the good intention of those who want to genuinely liberalise the market and reduce organised crime, but all we could be doing is exchanging the greed of criminals for the greed of some large corporations.**

My Views on Legalisation

If we look at the wider issue of drugs, there can be little doubt that drugs generally are a major international problem. Apart from the dreadful violence and crime it generates, drug barons are controlling huge fortunes corrupting towns, cities and governments throughout the world. The United Nations Office of Drugs and Crime estimates that the illegal drugs industry is worth $435 billion each year and accounts for 50% of all international crime. It was the US President, Richard Nixon, who back in the 1970s declared a 'War on Drugs'; that war has clearly been lost. Drugs have become a dreadful scourge, wrecking people's lives and causing havoc to parents. The social and economic cost of drugs is, according to the 2017 HM Government's drug strategy, costing £10.7 billion annually, £6 billion for theft alone. Cannabis is a part of this huge problem and cannot be separated from it.

I am convinced that the public health of our citizens must be at the centre of any legislation to legalise cannabis or indeed any drug.

It is essential that any future legislation contains a statutory duty of the state to mitigate against the harm we know cannabis and other drugs can cause. The measure of any civilised society is its ability to protect its citizens from harm. Some people joke about health and safety but, without it, the UK would be a considerably more dangerous and unpleasant place to live. You only need to visit countries which do not have strong health and safety laws to see the increase in industrial accidents and scandals where pollution has poisoned hundreds, and sometimes thousands, of people because of scant regard for the health and safety of their citizens.

If the government decides to legalise cannabis, then it must accept responsibility for the harm we know it can, and will, do. Yes, civil liberties are paramount in a free society but so is the government's responsibility to protect its citizens from harm, especially the vulnerable. The government must ensure that the harm cannabis can cause to users, especially teenagers, is minimised as much as feasibly possible. This is going to require substantial investment in regulating the growing, sale and consumption of cannabis. It is also going to require an even greater level of investment in healthcare, and social support for those who develop long-term mental illness as a result of exposure to cannabis which is likely to increase if legalised.

For those who say, "Well it's their choice if they become ill, that's their fault," I would remind them we have not taken that attitude with smoking, drinking or gambling. We are a civilised society that shows kindness, empathy, understanding, and long may that continue!

So let me put my cards on the table - do I believe cannabis should be legalised? Not yet, and certainly not until society is geared up to absorb the impact cannabis will have on the lives of the teenagers, adults and their parents who will be affected by its use. Will cannabis be legalised? At some time, yes, but I hope with considerable thought and resources.

If, in the Future, the UK Legalises Cannabis, What Should Future Legislation Look Like?

Before any government decides to fully legalise cannabis it is essential that it first looks at the lessons from those countries that have legalised cannabis. Although not all countries are comparable because of culture and social differences, we can still look and see what lessons can be learnt in the few years that legalisation has taken place, and which of these are relevant to the UK.

As mentioned, the health and wellbeing the citizens of the UK must be at the centre of any future legislation. If the government uses 'Public Health' as the benchmark for success, then we might just tip the advantages of legalisation ahead of prohibition, and begin to reverse the damage cannabis and other drugs have inflicted on our communities.

The UK already has a very sophisticated understanding of recreational drugs, as has most of the rest of the western world. If we start to combine best practice of harm reduction of drugs, and the working experience of those countries that have legalised and decriminalised cannabis, then we could begin to get on top of this huge health and social issue.

I don't intend to try and go into detail on what a post-legalisation drugs policy should look like; that will require a team of experts. There are, however, a number of very basic components that I believe should be included:

Prevention - Support - Regulation (See appendix 1)

These three basic components are similar to those adopted to control smoking, where we have seen a dramatic reduction over the last 50 years. It has taken over 50 years for the calls to reduce smoking to have any real impact. This was, and to some degree still is, partly due to the tobacco industry fighting tooth and nail to protect their brands. According to the Australian Cancer Council, NSW, the first medical reports linking smoking to lung cancer began to appear in the 1920s. Many newspaper editors refused to report these findings as they did not want to offend tobacco companies who advertised heavily in the media. As recently as 2006, a US court found various tobacco companies liable for covering up the health risks and marketing to children! (Article in **'Public Health Law Centre': United States v Phillip Morris).**

Let's hope that it does not take another 100 years for the true dangers of cannabis to be fully understood by society, and that it does not take 100 years for drugs generally to become more irrelevant to society's needs. I should add that many pharmaceutical companies do give millions to NGOs (Non-Government Organisation's) to support their work and provide funding for health education programmes, including cannabis awareness. This, I firmly believe is one way forward. The UK Government along with NGO's, should work in collaboration with these hugely profitable companies to develop and support national cannabis awareness campaigns as well as support to families caught up in cannabis induced mental illness. We have seen how well the government can successfully work with pharmaceutical companies with the development of vaccines for covid, so we know it is possible. Having been involved with a number of pharmaceutical companies in the past, I am very much aware they can show a social responsibility and are prepared to act philanthropical - so, let's harness this important resource.

I firmly believe that we can substantially reduce the use of cannabis and drugs generally. It may take a generation or two but I am convinced it can be done if we taxpayers are prepared to invest in the resources and work with the private sector. We may not be able to eliminate drugs completely but we can, without doubt, reverse the current trend and make drugs less relevant in people's lives. But it won't just happen, we will need to develop smart, evidence-based strategies and a determination and commitment to stick with it, even though we know changing people's behaviour and social norms take time. But it can be done and, if we want to consider ourselves a civilised society, then it must be done.

Chapter 11: A Final Reflection

"It is not in the stars to hold our destiny but in ourselves."
William Shakespeare

The use of drugs to stimulate the body and mind goes back thousands of years. Archaeologists have found the remains of psychotropic drugs which they believe ancient civilisations used to communicate with the spirits. Gladiators used strychnine to improve their performance and dull the pain. In the 1960s, Tommy Simpson, who was one of Britain's leading cyclists with a reputation for never giving up, shocked the cycling world. It was during the 1967 Tour de France, Simpson was nearing the summit of Mont Ventoux and he had pulled away from his teammates determined to catch the frontrunners. He was almost at the top when he started to zig zag across the road. He then keeled over and died of a heart attack. Simpson had been taking performance enhancing drugs, causing his body to perform way beyond its natural ability - his heart simply stopped. This is a very extreme example of artificially pushing the body beyond its physical limits. Pushing the brain beyond its natural limits with mind-altering drugs such as cannabis is no different. Admittedly the chances of actually dying are rare but damaging the brain is not, as it isn't rare for athletes to do long-term damage to their bodies using steroids and other performance- enhancing drugs.

The danger of using artificial stimulants on the body has been known for hundreds of years, but proving the link has only been possible due to modern science. Thanks to scientists like Professor Sir Robin Murray and his team, and many hundreds of scientists around the world, we now know with reasonable certainty that the high levels of THC in cannabis are linked to psychosis, especially amongst young people whose brains are still developing.

Early intervention is key to helping children avoid illegal drugs. Introducing a child to some very basic drugs awareness, whether it's legal drugs or medicine in your bathroom, will help them to be able to talk more openly about drugs as they reach their teens. There are some superb programmes that parents can use which are not complicated and which most parents can follow. If parents were alert to the dangers of cannabis and drugs generally, and in the same way as parents teach their children about normal health and hygiene to their pre-teen children, then I am convinced it would have a major impact on helping to reduce the impact cannabis is having on our society. If children and young people, especially those at risk, are fully supported by schools, we then have a real fighting chance.

For the parents struggling with a loved one with cannabis-induced mental illness, there is hope out there; you are not alone - there are steps you can take. There are organisations you can reach out to that can help you and your family to find some peace and stability. Life can get a lot better. One key ingredient is going to be the need for supporters of cannabis to be open and honest, and warn parents and teenagers of its potential dangers. Admittedly it is only a minority of the 2.6 million users, but all the same that minority represents thousands of parents whose lives are being torn apart.

I met a young guy on the train a couple of years ago. He must have been in his late 20s. He caught my attention because he was rolling a joint. I asked him if he had been smoking cannabis for long; he said he had - mostly at weekends. I asked him why he smoked it. He smiled and said. "Because I enjoy it". He went on to say that smoking a joint was far better than filling his stomach with pints of beer and, besides, he could get chilled out a lot quicker smoking a joint than booze. I asked him if he thought it might be dangerous. "No more than drinking and certainly no more than smoking cigarettes," he replied. I asked him if he would recommend cannabis to my teenage grandson. He once again looked up, smiled and said, "Definitely not, I grow my own which is far less potent than the stuff on the streets. You need to know what you are buying. The stuff on the streets is definitely not for kids." That's the kind of honesty we need to have so young people can make an informed choice.

As a campaigner the last thing I want to do is to demonise cannabis users, All that will do is to build up greater resistance and division. If we are going to overcome future generations of young people risking disabling their minds, we need to have an open and grown-up debate. It is no good the less tolerant members of society throwing the weight of the criminal system at cannabis users. That has not worked. Equally we do not want the more free-spirited libertarians demanding open access to a plant with known dangers. It is a real conundrum but one I am certain is not beyond the wit of us humans to work out. We already have potential models to work with. What is required is a few cool heads and the will and courage of politicians to find an amicable way forward - which does exist.

Providing the government is not seduced by the spurious, self-interest of some big businesses, and start to listen to independent experts from both sides of the cannabis divide, I am confident that the plague of drugs that permeates all corners of our society could, within a few generations, be confined to the history books.

Epilogue: When Hope Flowers

(Sometime in early 2000) …. I took Steve to the pub last night. He downed two pints for every one of mine. Within an hour and 6 fags later he had managed to turn our corner of the pub into a scene that resembled the London smog. The young girl who was collecting glasses had to ask if there was anybody in there. Steve showed my mates his latest drawings which he had been doing at the local day-centre. Everyone was impressed. Steve thought they were crap, but was chuffed by the praise.

I went to bed late, cursing as I needed to be up early.
Steve put his head around the corner, "Do you really think my drawings are OK?" I said they were really excellent. A sparkle appeared in his eye. I closed my eyes, smiling to myself…. Steve is finally on the mend'.

Steve on the mend

Appendix 1

The three basic components the government should include in any future legislation to legalise cannabis:

1. Prevention

Influencing and changing people's behaviour through well-funded 'Educational Health Programmes' will be essential. As I mentioned in Chapter 6, this should involve encouraging parents to start talking about cannabis, and drugs generally, to their pre-teen children. It is essential that this is backed up with cannabis/drugs awareness programmes at schools, colleges and universities, all of whom should be working with parents when they identify a vulnerable student.

We have seen how effective the Government's FRANK campaign helped to reduce the numbers of young people using cannabis and, when the funding for FRANK was cut, we saw how cannabis use increased. So, it will be crucial for future Health Education programmes to be well funded and sustained - for decades, if necessary. In addition to education programmes, there needs to be targeted support for those parents struggling to communicate with their children. Family intervention programmes have been tried and tested for decades such as 'Sure Start Family Centres', which have helped and supported thousands of disadvantaged parents over the last 17 years. Programmes like Sure Start desperately need to be rolled out across the country. The investment will pay huge dividends in the long run. Schools must be given the funding to ensure that excluding children is a thing of the past and actively work towards inclusion. Not to off-load children from one school to another like unwanted rags.

2. Support

We now know that cannabis can harm people's health so, if the State is going to endorse its use, then it will need to take responsibility for all those who are harmed by cannabis, and take responsibility for the wider social impact of cannabis. The government will need to increase its investment in funding treatment programmes, family support, social housing, rehabilitation programmes and sheltered employment. They will need to make talking therapy and other psychological therapies more easily available as well as investing in more Community Support Workers, Community Psychiatric Nurses and Psychiatrists. Above all, the government is going to have to make substantial investments into Social and Health Care. Without such a commitment built into any future legislation, it would be totally immoral to legalise a substance knowing it will do harm and not to mitigate against that harm.

3. Regulation

It will be essential to have very robust regulations that are backed up by the law, and resources to monitor the legislation. The Government must be responsible for the growing, distribution, sale and use of cannabis and cannabis extracts, through very controlled licence arrangements. We cannot leave this to the hands of large corporations to play market forces with such a potentially dangerous substance; market forces cannot be trusted when the prime motivation is to maximise profits for its shareholders. Of course, we will need the private sector, but they should be limited to a small number of commercial companies strictly licensed to grow and sell cannabis.

The potency of cannabis should be tightly controlled with a limit on the levels of THC. Marketing should be tightly controlled; claims made by companies about its benefits must be fully backed up with published research and agreed by government scientific advisers. There needs to be an age limit - possibly 21 - bearing in mind the damage THC can cause to developing brains.

The tax revenue from the sale of cannabis should be used to fund prevention programmes as well as funding the associated Health and Social Care needs.

Criminals caught supplying and selling should be dealt with using the full force of the criminal justice system.

Acknowledgements

The first acknowledgement has to be to Sir Tim Berners-Lee, the inventor of the world wide web. I doubt whether I would have had the time and tenacity to have finished the book – so, Sir Tim, thank you.

My Family has to be the number one acknowledgment, especially Steve, my son, who agreed that I tell his story, Chris, my wife, who has been as solid as a rock during the dark days of Steve's illness, and who has encouraged and supported me in writing this book - correcting my spelling and grammar (due to my mild dyslexia).

Other acknowledgements include:
Bob Hammond, Sir Professor Robin Murray FRS,
Marjorie Wallace CBE, FRC Psych, Dr Mervin Rowlinson,
Professor David Kingdon, Bharat Mehta CBE, OBE,
Vanessa Hammond, Nigel Freer, Bert Johnson (former Chair of Rethink and President of EUFAMI), Gail Chalkley, Stephen Berrill,
Elizabeth Burton – Phillips MBE, Amy Anderson, David Hare,
Anna Golden, Sue Charlesworth, Melanie Hammond, Paula Dring,
Laura Johnson, Carla Harris-Marsh, Des Palmer MBE,
Philippa Lowe, Mark Winstanley, Stephen Berrill, Terry Henson,
Dr Brenda Morris, John Bowen, Sharon Keevins, Steve Wileman,
Amy Anderson, Trina Whittaker BEM.

I would also like to thank Routledge Taylor & Frances publishers for agreeing for me to use extracts from the chapter I wrote for Peter K Chadwick's book Schizophrenia: The Positive Perspective, ISBN: 978-0-415-45907-5).

First published in Great Britain in 2021, edition 1

Copyright © 2021 by Terry Hammond

All rights reserved. No part of this publication may be reproduced, distributed, or transmitted in any form or by any means, including photocopying, recording, or other electronic or mechanical methods, without the prior written permission of the publisher, except in the case of brief quotations embodied in critical reviews and certain other noncommercial uses permitted by copyright law. For permission requests, write to the publisher, addressed "Attention: Permissions Coordinator," at the address below.

The Mill, Mill Street
Packington, Ashby-de-la-Zouch LE65 1WL

Learn more about the author: www.terryhammond.org.uk

Ordering Information:
Quantity sales. Special discounts are available on quantity purchases by corporations, associations, and others. For details, contact the publisher at the address above.

Orders by UK trade bookstores and wholesalers. Please contact KangarooUK: Tel: (01530) 560177 or email: hello@kangaroouk.com.

Printed in the United Kingdom

Cover Image: Phil Stern

Whilst every effort has been taken in the preparation of this book, no responsibility for any loss occasioned to any person acting or refraining from any action as a result of any material in this publication can be accepted by the author or printer or anyone connected to this book.

Author note: The referenced details in this book were correct at the time of writing. Referenced information can change as website pages close or are updated.